DISCOVERY GUIDE
WALKING WITH GOD IN THE DESERT

The Faith Lessons™ Series
with Ray Vander Laan

DISCOVERY GUIDE
WALKING WITH GOD
IN THE DESERT

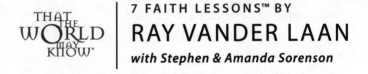

THAT THE
W**O**RLD MAY
KNOW®

7 FAITH LESSONS™ BY
RAY VANDER LAAN
with Stephen & Amanda Sorenson

ZONDERVAN®   FOCUS ON THE FAMILY®

ZONDERVAN.com/
AUTHORTRACKER
follow your favorite authors

ZONDERVAN

Walking with God in the Desert Discovery Guide
Copyright © 2010 by Ray Vander Laan

Requests for information should be addressed to:

Zondervan, *Grand Rapids, Michigan 49530*

Focus on the Family and the accompanying logo and design are federally registered trademarks of Focus on the Family, *Colorado Springs, Colorado 80995.*

That the World May Know and Faith Lessons are trademarks of Focus on the Family.

ISBN 978-0-310-32993-0

All maps created by International Mapping.

All photos are courtesy of Ray Vander Laan and Mark Tanis.

Interior design: Ben Fetterley

Printed in the United States of America

12 13 14 15 /DCI/ 25 24 23 22 21 20 19 18 17 16 15 14 13 12 11 10 9 8 7 6 5

CONTENTS

INTRODUCTION

From the beginning of human history, God the Creator planned to reclaim his world from the chaos of sin. He wanted to restore *shalom* to his creation, and he chose to use people to accomplish this divine purpose. Through the great exodus of the Hebrews from slavery in Egypt to their home in the Promised Land, God revealed himself to his people, gave them their identity as his chosen people, and instructed them in who he wanted them to become and how he wanted them to live.

So the exodus of the Hebrew people from Egypt to the Promised Land was more than a compassionate act of divine deliverance. It was God's calling of a people to be his "treasured possession," "kingdom of priests," and "holy nation" who would put him on display for the whole world to see (Exodus 19:4-6). God, in effect, took Israel as his bride, and lived among them through the years of discipline and testing in the desert in order to mold and shape them to be his faithful witnesses to the world.

And at the deepest level, the exodus story not only provides a background for God's plan to bring Jesus into the world as Messiah, it is one of the first chapters in God's great redemptive story to restore *shalom* — unity, harmony, order — to his broken creation.

For those of us who seek to live as God's people today, it is essential that we understand these stories as more than ancient history. The ancient stories of the Bible describe God and define the faith walk of his people. God's people come to know him by what he does, not by attempting to define him with precise doctrine. God's people come to live the way he desires by remembering, retelling, and reliving his great redemptive acts, not by simply memorizing laws, rules, and regulations.

Despite the many failures of God's people in fulfilling their role in that story, God's power has and continues to flow through his flawed (Jesus excepted, of course) human instruments to bring to fruition his plan of redemption. So, like the ancient Hebrews, we need deliverance from the bondage of Egypt. We need to be amazed by God's power at work at the Red Sea. We need to respond to his voice at Mount Sinai. As we wander through the deserts of our lives, we need to set our feet firmly on the foundation of depending on God and living by his every word. Their story is our story. As we come to know that story and partake of the redemption God offers through his Son, Jesus Christ, we too become part of that ancient story of redemption.

Thus the exodus is a paradigm for our own experience. As Christians today, we can describe our deliverance in similar language because God delivers us by his mercy and the protecting blood of the Lamb — Jesus Christ. Without the exodus, we would not be who we are — redeemed people delivered by the God of Israel. And without the hardships of the desert experience, we would find it difficult to learn how to live in intimate dependence on his provision and by faithful obedience to his every word.

The desert is one of the richest and most helpful images of the Bible. The beauty of the deserts of the Bible lands, the stories set there, and the people of the desert are deeply moving. Days spent in the desert are very hard. It's hot and there is no shade. The terrain is mountainous and very rugged.

Just walking through the deserts of the Middle East is difficult work. It leads desert travelers to wonder whether or not they can make it. But just when they feel they cannot go another step, God provides just enough of his presence — just enough shade, just enough water, just enough help from a fellow traveler to make it through the difficult places.

In the hardship and struggle to survive in the desert, we find a metaphor for surviving the desert experiences of heart and soul — the hard times of emotional, spiritual, physical, and relational pain that all of us face no matter where we live. We realize that life moves from one desert experience to another. The heat of our suffering during these times can be overwhelming. We may be weary and thirsty and find little or no refreshment. And yet, God is with us. He is our provider and our protector, and he will give us just enough. While no one looks forward to the desert experiences of life, knowing that in the heat of those desperate times God will provide just enough is hope enough to live significant and purpose-filled lives.

Clarifying Our Terminology

In this study, the record of God's reclaiming and restoring his broken world is called the Bible, Scripture, or the "text." Having studied in the Jewish world, I believe it is important to communicate clearly how the nature of that inspired book is understood. Although it can be helpful to speak of Scripture in terms of Old and New Testaments, these descriptions also can be misleading if they are interpreted to mean old and outdated in contrast to a new replacement. Nothing, in my opinion, is further from the truth.

Whereas the "New Testament" describes the great advance of God's plan with the arrival of the Messiah and the promise of his completed and continuing work, the "Old Testament" describes the foundational events and people through whom God began that work. The Bible is not complete without both Testaments; it comprises God's one revelation, his one plan to reclaim his world and restore harmony between himself and humankind. To emphasize that unity, I prefer to refer to the Hebrew text (Old Testament) and the Christian text (New Testament) that together are the inspired, infallible Word of God.

The geography of the lands of the Bible — Egypt, the desert, the Promised Land — shaped the people who lived there, and biblical writers assumed that their readers were familiar with the culture of that world. Many Christians today, however, lack even a basic geographical knowledge of the region and know even less of the ancient cultures that flourished there. So understanding the Scriptures involves more than knowing what the words mean. It also means becoming familiar with the everyday experiences and images the text employs to reveal God's message so that we can begin to understand it from the perspective of the people to whom it originally was given.

For example, the ancient Hebrew people to whom God revealed himself described their world in concrete terms. Their language was one of pictures, metaphors, and examples rather than ideas, definitions, and abstractions. Whereas we might describe God as omniscient or omnipresent (knowing everything and present everywhere), they would describe him as "my Shepherd." Thus the Bible is filled with concrete images from Hebrew culture: God is our Father and we are his children, God is the Potter and we are the clay, Jesus is the Lamb killed on Passover, heaven is an oasis in the desert, and hell is the city sewage dump.

Many of the Bible's images occur first during the exodus: Israel as God's bride, God as shepherd, the desert as a metaphor for life's difficult experiences, God as living water, God as king, God carrying his people on eagle's wings, the saving blood of the lamb. The Hebrews experienced these and many more familiar images as they left Egypt, spent forty years in the desert, and then entered the Promised Land.

The text frequently describes the people themselves, the descendants of Abraham, as "Hebrews," which probably originated from the Egyptian *habiru* meaning "dusty ones" (a reference to their desert origins). Genesis refers to Abraham as "the Hebrew" (Genesis 14:13), and after God gave Jacob the name *Israel*, the text also calls his descendants *Israelites*. The term *Jew* came into use later in history (see the books of Nehemiah and Esther) and was the predominant term used during the time of Jesus.

The Hebrew text refers to the land God promised to Abraham as *Canaan* or *Israel*. The Christian text calls it *Judea*. After the Second Jewish Revolt (AD 132 – 135), it was known as *Palestine*. Each of these names resulted from historical events that took place in the land at the time the terms were coined.

One of the earliest designations of the Promised Land was *Canaan*. It probably meant "purple," referring to the dye produced in the region from the shells of murex shellfish, the people who produced the dye, and the resulting purple cloth that was worn by royalty in the ancient world. In the Bible, *Canaanite* refers to a "trader" or "merchant" (Zechariah 14:21), as well as to a person from the "land of purple," or Canaan.

Israel, another designation for the Promised Land, derives from the patriarch Jacob. His descendants were known as the Hebrews or the children of Israel. After they conquered Canaan during the time of Joshua, the name of the people, *Israel*, became the designation for the land itself (in the same way it had with the Canaanites). When the nation split following the death of Solomon, the name Israel was applied to the territory of the northern kingdom, while the southern land was called Judah. After the northern kingdom fell to the Assyrians in 722 BC, the entire land was again called Israel.

During the time of Jesus, the land that had been the nation of Judah was called *Judea* (which means "Jewish"). The Romans divided the land into several provinces: Judea, Samaria, and Galilee (the three main divisions during Jesus' time); Gaulanitis, the Decapolis, and Perea (east of the Jordan River); and Idumaea (Edom) and Nabatea (in the south). About one hundred years after Jesus' death, the Roman emperor Hadrian called the land *Palestine* in an effort to eliminate Jewish influence in the area.

Today the names *Israel* and *Palestine* are often used to designate the land God gave to Abraham. Both terms are politically charged. *Palestine* is used by Arabs living in the central part of the country, and *Israel* is used by Jews to indicate the political State of Israel. In this study, *Israel* is used in the biblical sense. This does not indicate a political statement regarding the current struggle in the Middle East, but best reflects the biblical designation for the land.

Establishing the Historic and Geographic Setting for the Exodus

When studying the exodus of the Hebrews from Egypt, it is natural to ask, "When did that event occur?" or, "Who was the Pharaoh who did not know about Joseph?" (Exodus 1:8). Or "What route did they take to the Promised Land?" Significant textual and scientific support exists for more than one perspective on these questions. While I have my personal opinion on these matters, this study in no way argues for one position or another.

My foundational position is that the exodus and other biblical events occurred as the Bible describes them. My desire is to provide a sense of the culture of the time and place of these events without adding the burden of controversy regarding specific dates and locations. Thus I have chosen Ramses the Great as a model for the Pharaoh of the exodus because he was the epitome of all Pharaohs. I have chosen locations for this study that represent the type of terrain and culture that would be relevant no matter which route the Hebrews took.

The message of the Scriptures is eternal and unchanging, and the mission of God's people remains the same, but the circumstances of the people of the Bible are unique to their times. Consequently, we most clearly understand God's truth when we know the cultural context within which he spoke and acted and the perception of the people with whom he communicated. This does not mean that God's revelation is unclear if we don't know the cultural context. Rather, by cultivating our understanding of the world in which God's story was told, we will become more familiar with the world and culture of God's ancient people. We will better understand God's revealed mission for them so that we, in turn, will better understand God's purpose and more fully apply the Bible's message to our lives.

So come, I invite you to join me in walking in the dusty sandal prints of God's ancient people who walked and lived in these barren lands. The journey will not be easy, but I pray that you will learn that in the heat and struggle of the desert God is always just enough. I pray that you will discover the hope and faith that is birthed and sustained in harsh desert lands.

JOIN THE JOURNEY

During their forty years in the desert, Israel was transformed. The Israelites came out of Egypt as emancipated slaves with a vague remembrance of their God and little awareness of their identity. Through a journey of struggle and hardship made possible by the daily experience of God's ever-present love and provision, they came out of the desert as a people with a faith, a book, and a culture. No wonder the desert became a central theme in the faith life of God's people. It was not just a place through which they passed; it was how they gained a way of life, an identity; it was part of their very soul.

But the journey was not easy. The desert was a place of danger and death (Deuteronomy 8:15) compared to the safety of Egypt. In the desert, God's people experienced his protection more intensely because the threats were so severe — from poisonous snakes and scorpions, from enemies, from hunger and thirst. In that sense, the desert became a place of refuge and guidance where they experienced the shelter of God's protective care (Deuteronomy 2:7; Psalm 68:5 - 10).

The desert journey was also difficult because it revealed the true heart of God's people and their stubborn refusal to surrender completely to their God. It was a place of bitter resistance to God's leading and a selfish desire to return to the comforts of Egypt. So in the desert we see their bitter complaints about the lack of food and water (Exodus 15:22 - 24; 16:1 - 36; 17:1 - 7; Numbers 11:1 - 35; 20:1 - 13). We see their outright unfaithfulness and rebellion in the making of the golden calf (Exodus 32) and Korah's rebellion (Numbers 16). We see their unwillingness to take on the mission of reclaiming the Promised Land for God (Deuteronomy 1:26 - 36).

In the desert, God disciplined his people because they refused to continue the journey and become his holy people. As a result, the entire generation that had entered the desert died there. Their experience is a paradigm, a warning and a lesson, for every generation that resists God in order to serve its own desires.

But there is another side to the desert journey. It was also an awe-filled time when God revealed his presence in fire and cloud, when the thunder of his voice was heard. It was a time when daily miracles — water gushing out of rock, bread and meat from heaven — testified to God's love and protection of his people, his treasured possession. The journey in the wilderness was recalled as one of intimacy and faithfulness, when "as a bride you loved me and followed me through the desert" (Jeremiah 2:2). It was a wonderful time of intimate solitude with God when he forgave their sins and patiently molded them into the kingdom of priests and holy nation he desired (Exodus 19:6; Deuteronomy 8:2 - 5, 15 - 18).

The intimacy and intensity of Israel's worship in the desert was unparalleled in their history. It is true that they often rebelled and sinned grievously in the desert, yet they experienced God's loving provision anyway. They learned that he will chastise sinners but also offers unexpected redemption. Often God showed mercy to them in the desert because of his faithfulness to the covenants he made with their ancestors (Exodus 2:24; Leviticus 26:42; 19:5; 24:1 - 8) and with them. So they came to know him as a covenant God who is always faithful to his promises, even when his people are not.

The rich and personal nature of Israel's relationship with God was on full display in the desert. For generations into the future, when God seemed distant and his people were apathetic or defiant, the faithful returned to the desert. Some returned by remembering their ancestors' journey, others by going into the wilderness themselves. Going into the desert was for the purpose of restoring one's relationship with God — to relive a time when Israel, God's prized possession, fell in love with him in the desert. May our desert journeys — those difficult, confusing times of nearly overwhelming pain and hardship, punctuated with God's protective care and blessing — also lead us to rediscover our God and fall in love with him again.

Opening Thoughts (5 minutes)

The Very Words of God

> *In a desert land he found him,*
> *   in a barren and howling waste.*
> *He shielded him and cared for him;*
> *   he guarded him as the apple of his eye.*

Deuteronomy 32:10

Think About It

Imagine that you are in a stadium with tens of thousands of people watching a football game for the very first time — except there are no goalposts and you have no idea what the objective is. All you see is lots of running around, people crashing into one another, the ball being thrown first in one direction then another, and the spectators cheering wildly sometimes and seemingly devastated other times. How chaotic would that seem to you?

In what sense do our lives look a bit like that, particularly when we are going through a difficult time — what we might call a "desert" experience?

In football, when you add the goalposts and know the objective of the game, the chaos on the field starts to make sense. In life, what do you think helps us to begin to make sense out of the confusion and chaos of our difficult times?

DVD Notes (13 minutes)

God finds Israel in the desert

A place of danger and peril

A place of refuge and protection

Three lands—Egypt, Promised Land, desert

Learning to know, trust, and love God in the desert

God joins his people in the desert

DVD Discussion (10 minutes)

1. The exodus experience has had a profound impact on God's people. It was a turning point in God's unfolding plan of redemption. Through Israel's desert experiences during the exodus, God molded and shaped a people who would be his partners in restoring *shalom* (peace, harmony, unity) to his creation. So let's take a look at the deserts that have been so formative in the lives of God's people.

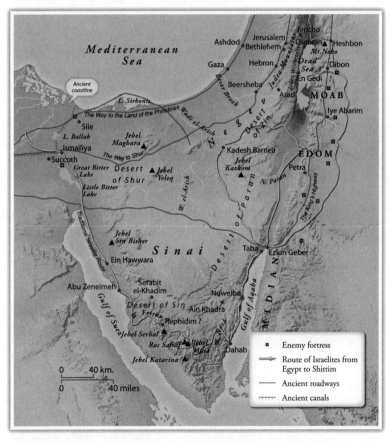

*Locate the **Sinai Desert, including the Desert of Sin and Desert of Paran.*** This is the "vast and dreadful" desert of the exodus. It is the most severe desert region with intense daytime heat, chilling nights, and little or no rainfall. Travel across it is difficult due to ridges of steep, rocky mountains.

The Desert of Paran, which extends into the Negev, is the general area where the Israelites wandered for forty years. Only God's miraculous provision enabled his people to survive there. This desert's inhospitable conditions are highlighted in Deuteronomy 1:19; 8:15 – 16 and Psalm 107:4 – 5.

*Locate the **Negev Desert, including the Desert of Zin.*** Barely forty miles south of Jerusalem, this desert has rolling desert pasture country in the north, rugged canyons in its central region that include the Desert of Zin, and extremely barren land that may receive only two inches of rainfall annually in the south. The nomadic patriarch Abraham, with whom God partnered so that "all peoples on earth" would be blessed (Genesis 12:1 – 3; 20:1), lived in the Negev along the edge of fertile farming areas to the north. He and his descendants Isaac and Jacob traveled great distances in the Negev seeking pasture and water for their flocks.

*Locate the **Judea Wilderness.*** This desert begins on the eastern slope of the Judea Mountains — roughly half a mile from the well-watered central mountains of Bethlehem and Jerusalem — and ends at the Dead Sea, approximately ten miles to the east. The steep, mountainous terrain descends suddenly from 3,000 feet above sea level to more than 1,400 feet below sea level at the Dead Sea in the Rift Valley. There is just enough rain along the western mountain ridge of this desert for shepherds to pasture their flocks, but the farther east one travels, the more arid the land becomes. Amazingly, this desert is within sight of most people living in Israel's central mountains. Its proximity to populated areas made it a refuge for those seeking solitude or safety. Here David hid from Saul, John the Baptist and the Essenes isolated themselves from the usual religious practices of the day in order to focus on God's words, and Jesus faced the evil one. Many biblical events occurred in this desert (1 Samuel 24:1 – 22; 26:1 – 25; Psalm 63).

2. What have you learned from this geographical overview of the desert regions of the Bible that helps you to better understand what was at stake or how some of the desert stories in the Bible unfolded, including the exodus and Israel's time in the desert?

3. Although the hardship and pain of the Israelites' time in the desert were all-consuming (as desert experiences tend to be), the whole experience was really about the bigger picture of what God desires to accomplish in the world. To what extent do you think the Israelites realized this at the time?

What light does their awareness, or lack of awareness, of God's greater purpose shed on how you perceive and respond to your own desert experiences?

4. How does knowing that desert experiences aren't just about the desert — that they are about God's purpose and presence in your life — give you a better perspective for enduring them?

5. How highly must God value his relationship with his people to lead them into the desert so that they come to know him intimately, depend on him completely, and obey him faithfully?

   What does this indicate to you about the connection between our desert experiences and our relationship with God?

6. How do you deal with the paradox of the desert — brutal hardship accompanied by the sweetness of God's presence, danger and peril accompanied by manna and living water, pain and suffering that accomplish God's purpose?

7. In what ways does the image of the exodus being about three lands — Pharaoh's land, God's land, and the Promised Land — give you perspective on your times in the desert?

Small Group Bible Discovery and Discussion (24 minutes)

The Paradox of the Desert

The desert is a land of paradox. It is a vast, rocky, barren wasteland, but where its few springs gush out of the rocks it is incredibly lush, beautiful, and refreshing. It is unbearably hot during the day and chillingly cold at night. And the Bible portrays Israel's experience as they journeyed through the desert from Egypt to the Promised Land as a paradox as well.

For the Israelites, the desert was a place of sin, rebellion, and punishment — the golden calf, their demand that God prove himself by providing water at Rephidim, their craving for the "good" food of Egypt, their revolt when they first approached Canaan. At the same time, the desert was a place where God mercifully provided for his people and drew them into an intimate relationship with him — leading them by his presence in pillars of cloud and fire, feeding them with manna for forty years, protecting them from physical harm, taking Israel as his treasured bride. So let's take a look at some of their desert experiences and see what we can learn that will help us to walk through the extremes and confusion of our own desert experiences.

1. When the exodus was coming to an end, what did Moses say was God's purpose for leading his people into the desert after he had delivered them from Egypt? (See Deuteronomy 8:1 – 5.)

   What difficulties did God bring upon his people, and how did he care for his people at the same time?

What do you think might be God's purpose in leading his people into desert experiences today?

2. What kind of a relationship did God want to have with his people, and what was required of his people for this kind of relationship to develop? (See Exodus 19:3 – 6.)

3. Life in the desert was difficult for the Israelites. We see clearly their struggle to survive that time and to learn to trust God and become the people he desired them to be. They would obey for a time, then rebel against God and what he was accomplishing through their desert journey. But always, even when he punished them because of their sin, God was faithful to live among his people and provide everything they needed. Read Psalm 78:10 – 54; Ezekiel 20:6 – 20; and 1 Corinthians 10:1 – 11, and for each discuss the following questions.

    a. In what ways were the Israelites dissatisfied with God's provision and unimpressed by his miracles?

    b. In what sense might we respond the same way when we are going through desert experiences?

   c. What impact did God want his miraculous provision to have on his people, and what finally got their attention?

   d. What do you think is the key to noticing what God may be trying to teach us when we go through desert experiences?

   e. How did the Israelites' sins affect their relationship with God, and how he continued to treat them?

   f. What greater purpose was God accomplishing through their desert experiences, and why is it so important?

4. Despite the sins of his chosen people, how did God prove himself faithful in the desert, and what did he at last accomplish? (See Psalm 77:11 – 20; Jeremiah 2:1 – 3.)

    Do you think this is what God wants to accomplish through our desert experiences as well? Why or why not?

5. Why is it important for God's people to remember what
    takes place in the desert? (See Psalm 78:1 – 8.)

6. The desert is characterized by brutal heat, intense thirst,
    frigid cold, scorching sun, and no shade. The path on which
    God leads us through life is at times like a desert too. The
    hardships of struggle, suffering, and pain that we face can
    overwhelm us as surely as harsh desert conditions do. As you
    answer the following questions, consider in what sense God
    is with us and helps us in our deserts.

    a. When the heat of hard times overwhelms us, what is
        God like for us? (See Psalm 121:5 – 7.)

    b. When we are desperately thirsty and need to quench the
        pain of our suffering, what will God be for us? (See Jer-
        emiah 2:13; 17:13; John 4:10.)

    c. When we hunger for the strength to keep going under
        the crushing burden of pain, what will God do for us?
        (See Psalm 105:40.)

    d. When have you seen God be shade, living water, and the bread of heaven for those who are suffering through a desert experience?

7. In what ways is Isaiah's description of what God will do for his people in the desert what we want and need in the desert as well? (See Isaiah 49:10.)

Faith Lesson (7 minutes)

It was a warm March day, and the sun streamed brilliantly through the classroom windows. When the bell rang, thirty-two high school sophomores headed out the door with far more energy than normal. It was the last day before spring vacation. Ahh! Ten days with nothing scheduled beyond the landscaping projects — one of my greatest joys — around my house. The weather forecast called for warm, sunny weather all week.

I (Ray) glanced at my watch: 2:55 p.m. I remembered my doctor's appointment at 3:20. I had postponed my annual physical for as long as my wife would let me. I hated physicals. They seemed so unnecessary and uncomfortably invasive for a healthy, fifty-five year old. I reached for my cell phone. Dr. Burns, a close friend, would understand if I postponed the appointment until after spring break. I had already gone to the laboratory and given all the samples they asked for. I could use the afternoon to buy plants and get an early start on my landscaping.

I hesitated, phone in hand. I had felt a bit fatigued for several months, but who wouldn't be tired with my schedule? I was over-scheduled with my teaching load, several seminars, and a video project in process. Now I had ten days to recover. With a sigh, I realized that I would be overwhelmingly busy for the next three months. Fitting in a doctor's appointment would make it even worse. I put my phone away, straightened the classroom, and headed out to my car.

I sat waiting for Dr. Burns. Maybe it was my eagerness to get to my flowers, but it seemed he was taking longer than usual. The exam had been routine enough. The stress test on the treadmill went well with both doctor and nurse impressed — or so they said — by my stamina and the time it took to bring my heart to the desired rate. That made sense. I'm not an athlete, but I had been a hobby runner for more than twenty-five years. I normally ran twenty-five or more miles every week, running three days then taking one off. I even kept a journal to make sure I maintained the discipline. Running gave me time to think and to memorize Scripture, a discipline I began two decades earlier. Besides, it relieved stress, kept my blood pressure normal and cholesterol down, and allowed me to eat what I wanted, especially meat.

Finally Dr. Burns came in, papers in hand. He sat down and placed the computer printout in front of us. With his usual efficiency, he reviewed the first pages: lab tests, cholesterol, and chest X-ray were all as they should be. Placing the stress test printout in front of me, he circled several of the peaks and valleys, looked at me for several moments, and then said in a quiet voice, "There is a problem here. The EKG shows you may have had a previous heart injury. As soon as possible we need to schedule further testing to look at your coronary status."

"Injury? That means a heart attack?"

"That is possible."

At that moment I felt strangely cold and alone in that small room, alone in the world. Everything seemed distant. My first reaction was to wonder if I could still plant my flowers. Numbly, I went through the motions of finishing the consultation. Dr. Burns said he would pray for me and would be involved each step of the way. I left his office and started home. *Heart attack? I'm fifty-five and healthy.*

I pulled into a parking lot and called my wife, Esther. "How did it go?" she said.

"He thinks I may have had a heart attack" I responded, unable to determine how I felt. Her response, with the faith I have come to expect from her, was quiet and encouraging. At that moment it didn't really matter. I looked into the rearview mirror at my reflection. "I'm broken. Why? What is going to happen?"

My much-needed vacation was a blur. I planted few flowers. There was an echocardiogram, X-rays, blood tests, and an angiogram. I watched, sedated but aware, as the young cardiologist showed my heart on a screen above us. "The left main trunk is 50 percent occluded and the left anterior is 100 percent occluded." Those words meant little, but I could see the dark line of one artery suddenly stop halfway down my heart. "You are fortunate," he continued. "It would not take much for this heart to be finished." I did not tell him I ran five miles the day before my physical.

Friends arranged for a consultation with a top cardiac surgeon at the Meijer Heart Clinic. A blunt-speaking man, he simply said, "I recommend a triple bypass. If we have caught this in time, I think I can restore most of the function. But your life will have to change." It already had.

During the following two weeks, I occasionally asked, "Why?" I had always taken care of my health (aside from far too much saturated fat, as I would learn), and there was no family history. Why coronary artery disease? My teaching ministry was in great demand, and God was blessing it beyond my wildest expectations. I was in production on two more video programs. I had been conducting five or more seminars in Israel annually that were known for their physical rigor. Why a heart attack when my ministry was reaching so many? I had eleven grandchildren that were the joy of my life. Why heart disease when they needed their grandfather?

Although I asked why, the experience was not a crisis of faith for me. I realize that many people in similar or much more difficult situations experience a crisis of "Why?" There is nothing wrong with asking the question, but for the most part I did not need to know why. For me, the much bigger and more difficult question was "How?" *How* will I get through this? *How* will Esther and the kids handle this if I do not make it? *How* will I continue my ministry? *How* will my life be if God spares me? *How* will I handle the pain if I come out of surgery? I did not know how to walk the path I was on, and I was scared. Some days the stress overwhelmed me.

April 15 is no longer income tax day for me; it is bypass surgery day. I awoke feeling like I had been hit by a truck, as they said I would. The surgeon said, "I think I gave you your heart back. If you don't take care of it, don't come crying to me." Praise God we caught the disease before my heart was seriously damaged. The surgery was successful, but days of pain, weeks of weakness, and months of rehabilitation followed.

God is so good. With a radical new diet, some amazing medication, a renewed dedication to fitness, and a whole team to help reduce the stress in my life, I'm doing well. But the year coronary artery disease took from my life was by far the hardest and most difficult time I have ever experienced. It was painful, frightening, frustrating, lonely, and a constant struggle in the unknown. My life turned upside down. I was in the desert. The heat was unbearable at times and the cold at others. I was overcome by thirst in a land with no water. I asked *why*, but received no answer. In that desert God was — directly and through others — shade and living water for me.

I know that I am not alone in having faced difficult desert experiences. As a teacher in a Christian school, I have seen many other people face their own desert experiences — a promising young man who took his life; students who followed Jesus but got caught up in addictions or other destructive life patterns; an exceptional, vibrant, and godly young man killed unexpectedly in a traffic accident in front of his own home; students who have died of cancer. Even as I write this, a former student, a godly wife and mother with three children, is on her way to Mayo Clinic. By God's grace, she has defeated breast cancer twice, but now the cancer has spread to her spine.

I have never learned *why* any of these things happened. But I have seen the miracle of God's provision and the profound molding of lives of faith of some who have suffered in these deserts. All who have walked the desert paths could testify to the exquisite suffering deserts bring. Many would bear witness to the amazing provision of manna from heaven, water from the rock, and shade from the brutal heat. That is what God's ancient people learned when God *led* them into the desert on the way to the Promised Land. It is what I learned in my own deserts.

The desert of my heart surgery and the remarkable way in which God met my deepest needs one moment at a time are the soil from which this study grew. It is my hope and prayer that it will encourage those of us who travel through desert lands to find God's remarkable provision in life's hard times. Although I don't know what your desert is, I do know that God is there. I know that through impossibly difficult circumstances he teaches, guides, and shapes us into the people he wants us to be — people who know him intimately, trust him fully, obey him faithfully, and by walking the path God sets before them help to bring a taste of God's *shalom* to their world.

1. What is your desert?

   What is the circumstance that you don't have the resources to overcome?

   What is the pain you cannot resolve or escape?

   What is the struggle that drags you down to the point that you don't know if you will survive to take another step?

2. As you walk the path through your desert, will you walk on
    your own, or join with God on that journey?

Will you walk your desert path with God and allow him to
be your provider, teacher, shepherd?

Will you seek to discover what it means to trust and depend
on him and get to know him as you have never known him
before?

Closing (1 minute)

Read together Isaiah 49:10: "They will neither hunger nor thirst, nor
will the desert heat or the sun beat upon them. He who has compassion on them will guide them and lead them beside springs of
water."

Then pray together, affirming your commitment to join God in the
desert and walk with him wherever your desert path leads.

Memorize

They will neither hunger nor thirst,
        nor will the desert heat or the sun beat upon them.
He who has compassion on them will guide them
        and lead them beside springs of water.

                                                    Isaiah 49:10

Walking with God through Our Deserts

In-Depth Personal Study Sessions

Day One | Living in a World of Chaos

The Very Words of God

> *For this is what the LORD says —*
> *he who created the heavens,*
> > *he is God;*
> *he who fashioned and made the earth,*
> > *he founded it;*
> *he did not create it to be empty,*
> > *but formed it to be inhabited —*
> *he says:*
> *"I am the LORD,*
> > *and there is no other.*

Isaiah 45:18

Bible Discovery

Desert: Only a Part of God's Story

God's story began in Genesis, when the earth was "formless and empty" — the opposite of God. As his Spirit hovered over the watery chaos, God spoke and by the power of his words formed and filled the chaos, imposing beautiful order onto disorder.

Everything God created was in perfect harmony (Hebrew: *shalom*) and he proclaimed that "it was very good" (Genesis 1:31). Then Adam and Eve, who were to be God's partners in maintaining and developing his magnificent creation, rebelled against him and violated his command. Chaos — disorder, meaninglessness, confusion, brokenness, death — was back, just as the evil one had intended. Humankind became separated from their holy God. Violence, cruelty, oppression, worship of false gods, pride, fearfulness, addictions — all these and more have become commonplace evidence that things are no longer as they are supposed to be.

Fortunately, God "is not a God of disorder but of peace" (1 Corinthians 14:33), and he is unfolding his plan to restore *shalom* to his creation. He created us for *shalom*, but we obviously don't live in paradise yet! Our world remains in chaos. So in the vivid, metaphorical language of the Bible, we experience seasons in life when we are in the "desert" — times of pain, suffering, and death. In the deserts of our lives, we become acutely aware of our longing for God and his *shalom*.

1. Read Genesis 1 - 2:3, especially 1:2 and 1:31, and describe in your own words the beautiful order — the perfect *shalom* — God imposed on chaos at creation. In what ways do you see yourself made to be a part of it, and in what ways do you long for it? (See Isaiah 45:18.)

2. What effect has the chaos that sin brought into God's creation had on people and their relationships with one another and with God? (See Genesis 4:8; Exodus 1:8 - 11, 15 - 16; 2 Kings 16:1 - 4; Isaiah 59:2 - 4, 7 - 16; Matthew 2:1 - 7, 16 - 18.)

    What kinds of deserts — pain, suffering, hardship — have people experienced because of it?

Which of these deserts have had a role in your life, and what impact have they had on you?

3. In Jeremiah 4:22 – 28, we read that God brought chaos back into the lives of his own people in response to their sin.

   a. In what ways was the destruction and ruin that God allowed a reminder of what the earth was like before creation?

   b. What metaphor is used to describe the chaos (v. 26), and what insight does this give you into the meaning of desert times in life?

4. After chaos destroyed God's magnificent order (Genesis 3), he began restoring *shalom* to his creation — and he is still doing that! What are some of the steps God has taken toward making things the way he created them to be? (See Genesis 6:5 – 7; 7:17 – 19, 23; 12:1 – 3; Exodus 19:1 – 6; Deuteronomy 6:1 – 9; Luke 2:8 – 12; 24:1 – 6; John 3:16; Hebrews 9:27 – 28; Revelation 21:1 – 4.)

When, even in the midst of your desert experiences, have
you seen at least a glimpse of what God is doing to restore
shalom to his creation?

Reflection

Pain, suffering, and struggle always point to the source of chaos:
sin, the violation of God's holiness that results from our own actions
or the presence of evil in the world. Until God completely restores
shalom to his creation, chaos will influence our lives. The biblical
metaphor of harsh, intense desert portrays this chaos in which we
experience disease, pain, poverty, violence, shattered relationships,
loneliness, oppression, and lack of meaning. In the desert, "natural"
disasters such as hurricanes, earthquakes, floods, drought, tornados,
and pollution occur. In the desert of the human heart, people vio-
late God's standards resulting in addiction, terrorism, war, sexually
transmitted diseases, innocent bloodshed, financial devastation, con-
sumerism, apathy toward people who suffer, selfish ambition, and
lack of time for family.

If we follow God, we live in two realities — that of sin, that of *shalom*. Adam and Eve sinned, civilizations have sinned, and each of
us has sinned. That is the world in which we live, the path we must
walk. Even those of us who have been forgiven and washed clean by
the blood of Jesus and walk toward the "promised land" of heaven
must deal with the chaos.

Yet God is at work bringing *shalom* to his creation in miraculous
ways. He walks with us in our deserts, bringing the *shalom* of his
presence and provision to us. We taste a bit of *shalom* as he answers
our prayers and brings encouragement for our journey through the
community of his people. Yes, the journey is still difficult and painful, but his presence will sustain us moment by moment, step by
weary step.

In what way(s) might your desert experiences be part of God's unfolding, redemptive story to restore his *shalom* to all things?

What hope does this give you in the midst of your pain?

What makes the chaos of your desert experiences especially difficult to bear?

In what ways has God's presence and provision given you a taste of *shalom* in the desert?

Memorize

> *We have this treasure in jars of clay to show that this all-surpassing power is from God and not from us. We are hard pressed on every side, but not crushed; perplexed, but not in despair; persecuted, but not abandoned; struck down, but not destroyed.*
>
> **2 Corinthians 4:7–9**

Day Two | Two Kinds of Deserts

The Very Words of God

> As Pharaoh approached, the Israelites looked up, and there were the
> Egyptians, marching after them. They were terrified and cried out to
> the LORD. They said to Moses, "Was it because there were no graves in
> Egypt that you brought us to the desert to die? What have you done to
> us by bringing us out of Egypt? Didn't we say to you in Egypt, 'Leave us
> alone; let us serve the Egyptians'? It would have been better for us to
> serve the Egyptians than to die in the desert!"
>
> *Exodus 14:10 – 12*

Bible Discovery

Desert as a Place and a Period of Time

What comes to mind when you hear the word "desert"? Wind-
swept sand and sun-bleached bones? Cacti? Snakes? Many of us
first picture a desert as a physical place, a geographic location that
has a name like Negev, Judea Wilderness, Mojave, or Sahara. These
deserts, although they are all different, have boundaries and certain
characteristics: water is scarce, there is little vegetation, and daytime heat can be overwhelming.

The Bible often mentions *desert* in the context of place. Moses met
God at the burning bush in the desert (Exodus 3:1 – 6). After leaving
Egypt, the Israelites walked into the desert (Exodus 15:22). David
ran into the desert to escape King Saul, and Elijah ran into the desert to escape Jezebel (1 Samuel 23; 1 Kings 19:1 – 4).

The Bible also mentions another kind of desert: a period of time
in life — brief or sometimes extended — during which we experience emotional, spiritual, relational, and/or intellectual pain. In this
sense, no matter where we live — an island rain forest or a city high-
rise — we all are desert people. These deserts are characterized by
the heat of pain, struggle, and suffering. During such times, we may
identify our pain as feeling like unquenchable thirst, our weariness
as brutal heat, and our struggles as a lack of bread.

1. While the Israelites struggled physically in the desert, in what sense did they also experience the desert of emotional and spiritual suffering? On the chart that follows, describe the suffering they experienced in both kinds of deserts. (See Exodus 14:1 – 4, 10 – 12; 15:22 – 26; 16:1 – 3; Numbers 11:1 – 15.)

Desert as a Place	Desert as a Period of Time

2. Why did God lead the Israelites into and through the desert for forty years, and how did he lead them? (See Deuteronomy 8:2 – 5; Psalms 77:20; 78:52.)

   In light of the fact that a desert shepherd leads by voice (and sheep will follow only their shepherd's voice), what does it appear that God wanted his people to learn about following him that they were likely to learn best in the desert? (See John 10:14, 27.)

In deserts of place, sheep who follow their shepherd's voice will be fed, watered, and kept safe from harm. What do you think God's people can expect when they follow God's voice through their desert experiences of pain, hardship, hunger, and danger?

3. What are some of the deserts David experienced during his life before and after becoming king of Israel? (See 1 Samuel 23:7 – 14; 30:1 – 10; 2 Samuel 15:13 – 17, 30; Psalms 3:1 – 2; 22:1 – 11; 32:1 – 7.)

Where did David consistently seek help — comfort, provision, protection — when he faced the deserts of his life?

What kind of relationship did David develop with God over time, and how great a role do you think his desert experiences played in his commitment to obeying God? (1 Kings 15:3 – 5.)

Reflection

In Deuteronomy 32:8 – 10, we read that God found Israel in a "howling waste." The word translated "waste," *tohu*, is translated in Genesis 1:1 as "formless." So there is a sense in which the desert is like the original chaos on which God imposed order. And while the desert — as a place or as a period of time — is desolate and painful, it is also where God meets his people and shapes and molds them as his instruments for restoring *shalom* to a broken world.

Many of us have never lived in a physical desert, although we may have driven through one. But all of us have lived in the desert of pain and suffering. Sometimes we do not know why we are in deserts of life; other times we know all too clearly. Regardless of why we are there, time in the desert gives us opportunities to gain a greater awareness of his sufficiency, renew our trust in and dependence on him, draw closer to him and listen attentively to his words, and choose to be more faithful in serving him each moment.

In which deserts have you lived, and why might you have experienced them?

What have been the hard lessons of those deserts, and how well do you remember them?

What have been the benefits and blessings of those deserts, and how meaningful are they in your life today?

In what way(s) have deserts shaped your life — in a sense "remade" you — into the person God wants you to be?

Memorize

> *Remember how the LORD your God led you all the way in the desert*
> *these forty years, to humble you and to test you in order to know what*
> *was in your heart, whether or not you would keep his commands.*
> *He humbled you, causing you to hunger and then feeding you with*
> *manna, which neither you nor your fathers had known, to teach you*
> *that man does not live on bread alone but on every word that comes*
> *from the mouth of the LORD.*

> *Deuteronomy 8:2 – 3*

Day Three | The Three Lands of the Exodus

The Very Words of God

> *He struck down all the firstborn of Egypt,*
> *   the firstfruits of manhood in the tents of Ham.*
> *But he brought his people out like a flock;*
> *   he led them like sheep through the desert....*
> *Thus he brought them to the border of his holy land,*
> *   to the hill country his right hand had taken.*
> *He drove out nations before them*
> *   and allotted their lands to them as an inheritance;*
> *he settled the tribes of Israel in their homes.*

> *Psalm 78:51 – 52, 54 – 55*

Bible Discovery

Living in the Lands of the Exodus

The exodus began in Egypt, the land of Pharaoh, which in Hebrew is *Mitzrayim*, meaning "bondage." Egypt is where God's people were not only enslaved physically but had chosen the bondage of trusting in Pharaoh and Egypt's gods to provide security, fertility, food, protection, guidance, and moral standards.

The exodus continued in the barren desert (Hebrew: *midbar*), which is, in a sense, God's land. In the desert, God joined his people on their journey, gave them his words, established an intimate covenant with them, and provided for their needs. For forty years God trained his people through difficulty and struggle to depend on him completely as their Shepherd and to live as his treasured possession.

The exodus ended in the Promised Land, the inheritance God gave to his people to use in obedience to him. In this blessed land — *their* land — God's people were to continue trusting him for everything they needed, to reject false gods, to give him credit for their blessings, and — most important — to live as God's "holy nation" that would demonstrate his *shalom* to the world.

In a sense, these three geographic regions represent the story of all God's people. As you discover how each of these "lands" played a role in Israel's story of redemption, consider how they play a role in your story as well.

1. What type of bondage did the Israelites experience in Egypt? (See Exodus 1:11 – 16; 16:3; Ezekiel 20:7 – 8.)

   In what ways might God's people today be in bondage without even realizing it?

2. During the years God spent leading his people in the desert, what did he desire to accomplish in their hearts and lives? (See Exodus 19:4 – 6; Deuteronomy 4:10 – 14.)

   To what extent was God successful? (See Jeremiah 2:2; Hosea 9:10.)

What perspective does God's purpose for leading the Israelites into the desert provide for understanding the role of desert experiences in the lives of God's people today?

3. How committed is God to restoring *shalom* in the hearts and lives of his people, and how does he do it? (See Hosea 2:13 – 23.)

How do we tend to view God's intent for our desert experiences, and how might it differ from his perspective? (See Hosea 2:14, 19 – 20, 23.)

Given God's intent for our desert experiences, how frequently might we find ourselves in the desert?

4. Just before the Israelites entered the Promised Land, what did God repeatedly remind them to do and why? (See Deuteronomy 4:5 – 8; 6:1 – 12; 8:6 – 20.)

How well did they remember? (See 2 Kings 17:9 – 17; 2 Chronicles 28:22 – 25; 36:11 – 14.)

Reflection

Although the story of the Israelites and their exodus from Egypt to the Promised Land occurred long, long ago, its plot parallels the plot of our life's story if we are followers of Jesus. We have been freed from the bondage of sin, which includes relying on anything or anyone other than God. We will experience difficult deserts in life as God seeks to train us to depend on him and obey him always. When we experience days of blessing and abundance, God's wants us to remember him in praise and by faithfully obeying his every Word. And one day we will receive the promised land of our inheritance in heaven.

Take some time to reflect on your life's story in the lands of the exodus.

Egypt: In what ways are you (or have you been) "in bondage in Pharaoh's land" by trusting in someone or something other than God to provide for your needs?

Desert: How faithful are you to trust God completely when you experience desert times? What might God desire to teach you in the scorching desert that you might not be able or willing to learn any other way?

Promised Land: To what extent do you view your blessings — every one — as coming from God? What impact do you think God wants your desert experiences to have on your life after you are out of the desert?

Day Four | God Shapes His People in the Desert

The Very Words of God

Show me your ways, O Lord,
*   teach me your paths;*
guide me in your truth and teach me,
*   for you are God my Savior,*
*   and my hope is in you all day long.*
Remember, O Lord, your great mercy and love,
*   for they are from of old.*
Remember not the sins of my youth
*   and my rebellious ways;*
according to your love remember me,
*   for you are good, O Lord.*
Good and upright is the Lord;
*   therefore he instructs sinners in his ways.*

Psalm 25:4 – 8

Bible Discovery

God Teaches His People His Ways

The exodus was a pivotal event in the Israelites' story. Because it occurred in the harsh deserts of the Sinai Peninsula and Israel, desert has played a central role in their religious faith. In God's plan, the harsh desert was a place of training and learning, not a place of punishment. He led them into the desert knowing that they could not survive without his help and that even with his provision life would not be easy.

As God provided faithfully for his people and taught them to obey his words in the barren, scorching desert, they slowly — and painfully through much sinful rebellion, punishment, and forgiveness — became the people he desired them to be. They became the kingdom of priests and holy nation that God prepared to enter the Promised Land and take the next step in God's unfolding plan to restore *shalom* to his broken world. Most of the Israelites' later triumphs in God's service were rooted in their desert education.

1. Based on the following texts, what three key things did God desire his people to discover and learn through their time in the desert?

   Exodus 29:45 – 46

   Deuteronomy 5:32 – 33; 7:11; Psalm 78:5 – 7

   Deuteronomy 13:4; Psalm 81:13; Matthew 16:24

   How important do you think it is for God's people to learn the same things today, and how do we learn them?

2. In what ways did God lovingly provide for the Israelites
    in the desert, and what do you think they learned about
    God and themselves through his provision? (See Exo-
    dus 13:21 - 22; 16:4 - 5, 22 - 28; 17:1 - 6, 8 - 13; Numbers
    10:33 - 36; 21:4 - 9.)

    What have you discovered about God and yourself as a result
    of his care and provision for you during times of desert?

3. The Israelites' experiences in the desert transformed them
    from being oppressed refugees into a powerful nation called
    to display God's character to the world. God told them
    repeatedly never to forget their desert lessons. Remember-
    ing was vital to the identity and mission of his people — and
    it remains vital to his people today. What are some of the
    practices God instituted in the desert to build up the faith of
    his people and to help them to remember their commitment
    to walk on his path only? (See Exodus 12:12 - 14; 20:1 - 17;
    31:13 - 17; Leviticus 1 - 7; 16; 23; Numbers 6:22 - 27; Deuter-
    onomy 31:9 - 13.)

    How might it help you to walk faithfully with God if you
    established some regular practices that remind you what
    God has done for you during your life's deserts?

Reflection

Israel's desert experiences during the exodus were foundational in shaping them to be the people God desired them to be. Sometimes those experiences were difficult and painful. Again and again, the Israelites complained and rebelled against God and the leader he had chosen, Moses. Yet over time, they became passionately devoted to him.

Those of us who desire to walk with Jesus also are called to become God's people — wholly dedicated and obedient to him. And the best way for God to shape us is in the desert — the same way he shaped the Israelites. In the desert, we have an unprecedented opportunity to know God intimately as he provides for us and teaches us, step by painful step, to obey and follow him.

What have you learned about God and yourself during terribly difficult desert times?

Could you have learned these things any other way?

How thankful are you that God is faithful to work with stubborn and resistant people who learn so slowly?

How central to the development of their faith was the time the Israelites spent in the desert?

How central to the development of your faith has been your time in the desert?

What do you do to keep the memory and significance of your desert experiences alive?

Memorize

May God be gracious to us and bless us
*   and make his face shine upon us,*
that your ways may be known on earth,
*   your salvation among all nations.*
May the peoples praise you, O God;
*   may all the peoples praise you.*

Psalm 67:1 – 3

Day Five | Returning to the Desert

The Very Words of God

My heart is in anguish within me;
*   the terrors of death assail me.*
Fear and trembling have beset me;
*   horror has overwhelmed me.*
I said, "Oh, that I had the wings of a dove!
*   I would fly away and be at rest —*
I would flee far away
*   and stay in the desert;*
I would hurry to my place of shelter,
*   far from the tempest and storm."*

Psalm 55:4 – 8

Bible Discovery

Back to the Desert — to Remember

After Moses died, God used Joshua to lead the Israelites into the Promised Land, the "good land" they had heard about for so long. They left behind the brutal heat and waterless wasteland of the desert and enjoyed springs of fresh water and the Jordan River flowing through *their* land. They experienced the comfort of living in cities they had not built and eating food from trees and vines they had not planted. As they took possession of the land, they saw their God stop the Jordan River from flowing, drop Jericho's walls, stop the sun in its path across the sky, and rout entire armies.

But how faithful would they be in keeping the lessons of the desert? Sadly, things fell apart quickly. God's people became complacent about being faithful to God and obeying his words. They indulged in the pagan practices and worship of the false gods of the Canaanites. They somehow forgot God's commands to *remember* (Hebrew: *zakar*) the past — to learn from it and obey accordingly.

So God sent his prophets to call his people back to the desert. In some cases, the Israelites literally re-entered the desert in order to spend precious time alone with God. In others, they remembered the desert by reliving the ancient story of what their ancestors had experienced and learned in the desert.

1. What role was the desert intended to play in the lives of God's people? (See Isaiah 40:1 – 5; Hosea 2:14 – 15, 19 – 23.)

2. Many of Israel's faithful lived in the desert for periods of time (or longed to do so). Some of them went into the desert to hear God's words and prepare his way. Others longed for the intimate holiness of his presence. Still others found refuge in the desert. As you read the following texts, consider the reasons, difficulties, and rewards of each person's desert

experience. Consider too how your desert experiences may be similar.

Exodus 3:1 - 6

1 Samuel 23:14, 24 - 29; Psalms 18:1 - 2, 31 - 33; 63:1

Jeremiah 9:2

Matthew 3:1 - 3; Luke 1:80; 3:1 - 3

Matthew 4:1 - 11

Hebrews 11:32 - 34, 38 - 39

3. How strongly did God emphasize to the Israelites their need to "return to the desert" — to *remember* the lessons they learned there and to make sure they remained on his path? (See Numbers 15:37 – 41; Deuteronomy 4:9 – 14; 6:1 – 9; 31:9 – 13.)

In what way did Jesus reinforce to his disciples the importance of *remembering* when he was with them in the upper room before he was arrested and crucified? (See Luke 22:14 – 19.)

What are some ways we can relive those events with Jesus and his disciples as if we were there rather than simply recalling the historical facts of that evening?

Reflection

It is easy for us to equate God's commands to *remember* primarily with mental recall rather than with a vivid reliving of the ancient desert story. Yet God wants us to remember in the sense that we reexperience the events and discover what he taught and how his people put those lessons into practice. When we remember in that sense, God can shape and form us into the people he desires us to be.

Just as God commanded the Israelites to remember the desert, we are to remember it as well. We are to remember God's faithful provision of water and manna, protection and meat. We are to remember his hatred of sin. We are to remember the importance of not only hearing God's words but obeying them with every fiber of our being.

God longs for us to be rooted in him, to draw near to him in trusting dependence, and to delight in obeying his commands and receiving the fulfillment of his promises. As we experience our life's deserts, may God's provision through shade, water, manna, and protection become as real for us as it was for his ancient people in the desert. May God say of us as he did of the ancient Israelites who traveled desert paths long before us, "I remember the devotion of your youth, how as a bride you loved me and followed me through the desert, through a land not sown" (Jeremiah 2:2).

How might you benefit by studying intensely the Israelites' time in the desert and *remembering* what occurred as if you had been there — as if you had seen Pharaoh's army racing toward you by the Red Sea, as if you had stood in terror listening to God's words thunder out from cloud and smoke at Mount Sinai?

How might your view of, and reliance on, God change?

How might your desire to experience God grow?

How might your commitment to obey God's Word deepen?

How might "returning" to the desert by *remembering* keep you focused on God's powerful, redemptive, and healing work on behalf of his people — including you?

Memorize

For the LORD's portion is his people,
    Jacob his allotted inheritance.
In a desert land he found him,
    in a barren and howling waste.
He shielded him and cared for him;
    he guarded him as the apple of his eye,
like an eagle that stirs up its nest
    and hovers over its young,
that spreads its wings to catch them
    and carries them on its pinions.

Deuteronomy 32:9 – 11

IT'S HOT HERE AND THERE'S NO WAY OUT

For God's ancient people, the desert regions of Israel and the Sinai Peninsula were a vast expanse of rocky, mountainous terrain and deep, treacherous wadis. There was no escaping the harsh reality of life in these barren lands where even the necessities of water and food were scarce. God's people experienced scorching daytime heat, venomous snakes and scorpions, and cold nighttime temperatures. But even as his people experienced the hardships of desert life, God was there. When they were overwhelmed by needs they were powerless to meet, he met them in the desert and provided food, water, and protection.

God often used the challenging and painful circumstances of desert life to teach his ancient people to listen to his voice and to trust him — and only him — to provide everything they needed. Through his faithful provision in the midst of their desert experiences, God formed a people who knew him intimately, trusted him fully, and lived in dependence on his every word. In fact, the Jewish sages have noted that the beautiful image of love portrayed in the Song of Songs, "Who is that coming up from the wilderness, leaning on her beloved?"[1] also described Israel, God's people, as they came out of the desert.

So it is not by chance that many notable servants of God mentioned in the Bible — Abraham and Sarah, Isaac and Rebekah, Moses, Joshua, David, Elijah, John the Baptist, Jesus, and Paul — all spent significant time in the desert before rising up to fulfill their roles in God's plan of redemption. It is not by chance that before the Israelites entered the Promised Land they too spent time in the desert.

There, through God's faithfulness, they learned to rely on his love and provision as they faced the challenges and uncertainties of fulfilling their intended purpose.

And it is not by chance that God's people today, although we may never set foot in a physical desert, go through "desert" experiences — intense times of struggle and pain, uncertainty and lack of control that push us to the end of our resources and abilities. God has not changed his ways when it comes to forming his people. He still uses deserts — difficult as they are — to lead us to the place where we choose to depend on him and his provision rather than trusting in ourselves. And when we make that choice, he meets us in our deserts just as he met his ancient people in their deserts.

So let's take a closer look at the deserts of our lives. Let's see what God provides when difficulties threaten to overwhelm us, when the temperature soars and we are powerless to deliver ourselves. Let's choose to discover the God who meets us there so that we may grow into a deeper, more intimate relationship of trust with him. May we too come out of our deserts leaning on our Beloved.

Opening Thoughts (3 minutes)

The Very Words of God

> I lift up my eyes to the hills —
> > where does my help come from?
> My help comes from the LORD,
> > the Maker of heaven and earth.
> He will not let your foot slip —
> > he who watches over you will not slumber;
> indeed, he who watches over Israel
> > will neither slumber nor sleep.
> The LORD watches over you —
> > the LORD is your shade at your right hand.

Psalm 121:1 – 5

Think About It

When life goes well, it is easy for us to feel confident and in control. It is easy to believe that our own decisions and actions will provide what we need and produce the outcomes we desire. At other times, life doesn't go as well as we would like. We may face times of struggle and pain — times of "desert" in our lives — when we are not sure how things will turn out and our confidence in successfully facing what lies ahead falters.

What impact do you think a person's relationship with God has on how he or she handles the deserts in life? What impact have you seen desert times have on your own relationship with God and your expectations of how he will respond to your needs?

DVD Notes (29 minutes)

God brings his people into the desert

God meets us during our "desert" moments

Walking by faith on God's path

The shade God provides

The shade God's people provide

DVD Discussion (7 minutes)

1. This study was filmed in Wadi Nasb in the Sinai Peninsula. An ancient caravan route passed through this wadi that connected the coastal road along the Gulf of Aqaba to the interior desert regions of the Sinai Peninsula.

    On the map on page 59, locate Jebel Musa (the traditional Mount Sinai) and Wadi Nasb. Then locate the Desert of Paran, Desert of Zin, and the Negev, the desert regions through which God led the Israelites for forty years before he allowed them to enter the Promised Land. If you have the resources to do so, look up satellite images of these desert lands to add to your understanding of what it would be like to live in this vast, rugged terrain.

2. In what ways did the view of the desert wilderness presented in the video help you to better understand what the writers of the biblical text may have envisioned when they described living in relationship with God as walking by faith, not by sight?

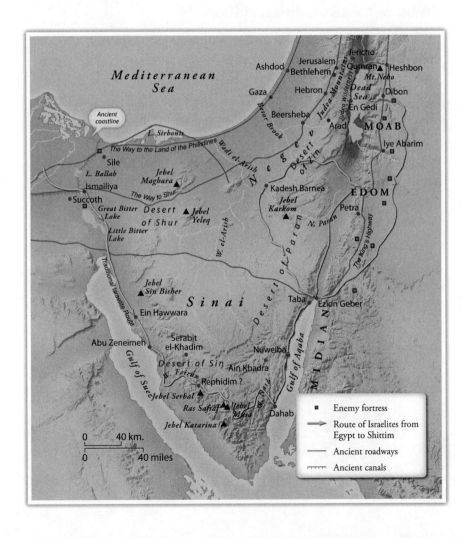

DID YOU KNOW?
Hardships and Dangers in the Desert

Because most of us may be unfamiliar with Middle Eastern geography, it's easy to underestimate the difficulties that Moses, the Israelites, and others experienced in the deserts of the Sinai Peninsula and the Trans Jordan region. We may picture the Israelites' exodus from Egypt as a journey across flat, sandy plains covered with sparse vegetation. But in these desert regions, steep, rocky mountain ranges surround and crisscross the flatter valleys and plains, making travel much more difficult. Just imagine how difficult it would have been for the Hebrews to pass through the granite and sandstone mountains of the southern Sinai!

In addition to the difficulties of traveling through unforgiving terrain, the deserts of the Bible receive little rainfall. The Negev receives about ten inches annually; the Wilderness of Paran and Judea Wilderness receive less than two inches. Yet the sparse rainfall is deceiving. Nearly all of the rainfall in the mountains to the north and west of these deserts falls during the six-month rainy season. The hard stone and meager topsoil of the mountains cannot absorb all of the rain, so it runs west toward the Mediterranean and east and south into the deserts. Rain in the desert often falls heavily for short periods of time, adding to the streams that rush quickly down the mountains and carve deep flood canyons that open into the valleys below.

A desert flood canyon, called by its Arabic name, *wadi* (*nahal* in Hebrew, often translated "brook" or "stream" in English),[2] is normally dry and may

be used as a road. The road from Jericho to Jerusalem, for example, passes through the Judea Wilderness alongside a deep wadi. In Wadi Nasb, where this study was filmed, an ancient caravan road led from the interior deserts of the Sinai Peninsula to the coastal road along the Gulf of Aqaba. The route is still used today.

However, wadis can flood suddenly, even when there isn't a cloud in the sky. From some trails in these narrow riverbeds it is impossible to see more than a few hundred feet ahead or behind, so travel through a wadi can be dangerous. In fact, even today, as was true centuries ago, the greatest cause of death in

IN THE DESERT WADIS, THE VIEW OF WHAT LIES AHEAD IS LIMITED AND ESCAPE FROM SUDDEN FLOODS MAY BE IMPOSSIBLE.

Middle Eastern deserts is not heat or thirst but floods in the wadis. So traveling into the unknown desert territory was difficult for the Hebrews. They had to trust God and his servant, Moses, to protect and provide for them no matter what danger or hardship might be ahead. Passing through the "deserts of life" is not easy. It has always been difficult for God's people—and it still is.

3. What kinds of desert experiences in life push us to the edge of our self-sufficiency?

When you face trouble in one of life's deserts, what does it mean to you when God steps in and meets you at a point of great need and demonstrates his loving care for you?

What impact does his presence during times of trouble have on your relationship with him?

4. When you feel overwhelmed in one of life's deserts, what kind of "shade" do you expect God to provide for you?

In what ways might your image of shade differ from the reality of the shade provided by a broom tree in the desert?

To what extent does God's provision of "just enough" shade for the day satisfy your desire for relief from the hardships of life in the desert?

Which personal story of God providing shade during a desert in your life might you want to share with the group?

Small Group Bible Discovery and Discussion (16 minutes)

God Wants His People to Rely on Him

God knew that his chosen people would be driven by the desire to provide for themselves and pursue their own ways if they did not learn to completely depend on him for guidance and direction, provision and protection. So he forced them to leave the lush, fertile lands of Goshen where they had irrigated their crops with the waters of the Nile River and enjoyed abundant harvests. He led them into the unknown, barren deserts of the Sinai Peninsula where they would have to depend on him and trust in him in order to survive.

1. Exodus records a number of desert situations in which the Hebrews revealed what they *really* believed about God and Moses, his chosen leader. As you read about three of these situations, notice how God used each one to teach his people that they could depend on him to meet their needs.

Text	What hardship or crisis did they face?	What was their "solution"?	How did God show himself to be a trustworthy provider?
Ex. 15:22–27			
Ex. 16:1–5, 9–15			
Ex. 17:1–6			

In these instances the desert, with its limited sources of food and water, was exactly the place into which God had led his people. Why do you think he led his people into a strange, unknown place that would be difficult, dangerous, and frightening?

What do you think his purpose might have been in not revealing ahead of time what to expect or how he would provide?

What do you think God might want us to experience and learn when we face unknown, unpredictable, and frightening deserts in our lives?

2. Before the Israelites entered the Promised Land, Moses spoke to them about all that they had experienced during their desert journey so that they would remember it when they lived in the good land God had provided for them. Deuteronomy 8:1 – 5 and 11:2 – 15 give us insight into God's intended purpose for the hardships of the Israelites' desert experience. As you read these portions of the text, note the contrast between our human drive for self-sufficiency and how God wants us to depend on him.

a. What do people really want in life, and how did God
    intend for his people to receive it? (See Deuteronomy 8:1.)

b. What process did God use to expose the self-sufficiency
    of his people and to provide for their needs, and in what
    ways is it similar to what he does through our desert
    experiences today? (See Deuteronomy 8:2 – 5.)

c. How had God taught his people that he was sufficient —
    that he was their provider? (See Deuteronomy 11:2 – 7.)

d. What impact did God expect his provision in the desert to
    have on his people, and what would their faithful trust in
    him produce for them? (See Deuteronomy 11:1, 8 – 9.)

e. What direct contrast related to self-sufficiency did God
    draw between the land of Egypt and the Promised Land?
    (See Deuteronomy 11:10 – 15.)

    f.   To what extent do you think the desert experiences in our lives help to expose our inclination toward self-sufficiency?

3.   Generations after the Israelites entered the Promised Land, what did God, through his prophet Jeremiah, lament about the hearts of his people? (See Jeremiah 2:13.)

What impact does our stubborn inclination to pursue our own ways and place confidence in our own self-sufficiency rather than in God's provision have on our relationship with him? And on our future well-being?

What are the "cisterns" we dig for ourselves today?

Faith Lesson (4 minutes)

Many of us who live in economically prosperous cultures consider God's blessings to be the things that make our lives easier, more pleasurable, and predictable. We put a great deal of effort into avoiding situations or conditions that would make life harder, less pleasurable, and less predictable. We have ten-year plans, insurance for every possible peril, and retirement accounts because we want the security of having in hand everything we could possibly need or want for tomorrow. And then, when our plans and resources fail to protect us from hardship, we may view the situation as God's judgment on us.[3]

In contrast, God often leads his people into harsh and painful deserts where life is not predictable, where we cannot store away everything we may want or need for the future. Deserts expose the fallacy (and sinfulness) of our self-sufficiency and force us to face the unknown. At that point of powerlessness, we make a crucial decision: will we learn to depend on God for each day's protection and provision, or will we choose our own way?

1. In Luke 12:13 – 21, Jesus told a parable about a person who was unable to see around the next bend of life yet trusted in his resources and ability to provide for himself.

   a. How does this parable help you put your self-sufficiency into perspective?

   b. In what ways have deserts — perhaps the loss of your job, home, retirement income, health, significant relationship, or your failure to achieve a desired goal — destroyed your comfortable self-reliance and forced you to reconsider your perspective on what you control and where you place your trust?

   c. In what way(s) has your experience in the desert changed how you trust and rely on God?

2. In what way(s) might God be leading you (or someone you know) into the unknown — into a desert?

How does what you have discovered during this session encourage you to view whatever difficulties lie ahead as opportunities to meet God, learn his ways, and experience him more intimately?

Closing (1 minute)

Read Deuteronomy 11:10 - 15 together: "The land you are entering to take over is not like the land of Egypt, from which you have come, where you planted your seed and irrigated it by foot as in a vegetable garden. But the land you are crossing the Jordan to take possession of is a land of mountains and valleys that drinks rain from heaven. It is a land the LORD your God cares for; the eyes of the LORD your God are continually on it from the beginning of the year to its end. So if you faithfully obey the commands I am giving you today — to love the LORD your God and to serve him with all your heart and with all your soul — then I will send rain on your land in its season, both autumn and spring rains, so that you may gather in your grain, new wine and oil. I will provide grass in the fields for your cattle, and you will eat and be satisfied."

Then pray, asking God to reveal to you areas of your life in which you trust in yourself and pursue your own ways rather than trusting in him and his faithfulness.

Memorize

The land you are entering to take over is not like the land of Egypt, from which you have come, where you planted your seed and irrigated it by foot as in a vegetable garden. But the land you are crossing the Jordan to take possession of is a land of mountains and valleys that drinks rain from heaven. It is a land the LORD *your God cares for; the eyes of the* LORD *your God are continually on it from the beginning of the year to its end. So if you faithfully obey the commands I am giving you today — to love the* LORD *your God and to serve him with all your heart and with all your soul — then I will send rain on your land in its season, both autumn and spring rains, so that you may gather in your grain, new wine and oil. I will provide grass in the fields for your cattle, and you will eat and be satisfied.*

Deuteronomy 11:10 – 15

Walking with God through Our Deserts

In-Depth Personal Study Sessions

Day One | When We Cannot See the Way

The Very Words of God

> Let the morning bring me word of your unfailing love,
>   for I have put my trust in you.
> Show me the way I should go,
>   for to you I lift up my soul.
>
> *Psalm 143:8*

Bible Discovery

We Can Be Confident of God's Watchful Care and Guidance

As they journeyed across the desert on ancient trails that led over steep, rocky ridges and through deep, twisting wadis, the Israelites often could see only a short distance ahead. This fit perfectly into God's plan. He seldom reveals the future to those who follow him. Rather, he demonstrates his daily provision as his people experience the pain, fatigue, and uncertainty of desert circumstances.

In harsh, unforgiving desert environments, we can experience what being in an intimate relationship with a loving, forgiving, compassionate, and faithful God means. But such a relationship doesn't come easily. Our first inclination is to choose our own path and trust in our own strength. When those resources fail, when we face danger, grow weary, or lose our way, God is faithful to protect, strengthen, and guide so that we learn to draw near to him and rely on him with confidence.

1. The Hebrews had camped at Mount Sinai for nearly a year. They had experienced the intense reality of God's presence as he established an intimate, covenant relationship with

them. Then he commanded Moses, following the cloud of God's glory, to lead the people into the desert toward the Promised Land — a destination none of them had seen. As they started out, how confident were they of God's provision in the unknown desert ahead versus the self-sufficiency they had experienced in Egypt? (See Numbers 10:33; 11:1 - 6.)

When have you faced times of uncertainty that tested your confidence in God's watchful guidance and provision?

How strong was the temptation to rely on someone or something other than God during those times?

How great a price were you willing to pay for whatever "security" you could grasp to lessen the risk of what might be ahead?

IN SOME DESERT WADIS, THE VIEW OF WHAT LIES AHEAD IS LIMITED.

What did you learn during those times of uncertainty about trusting God for the unknown path ahead?

2. When the future is uncertain, nearly all of us will go to great lengths to try to meet our own needs. Yet God, who is always faithful, has promised to meet the needs of everyone who relies on him. The following portions of the Psalms provide a picture of God's character and commitment to his people. As you read them, consider how knowing God intimately would give his people — in ancient times and today — confidence to face the unknown.

Psalm	God's people can face the unknown because God ...
9:10	
20:6–8	
23:1–6	
89:8, 13–18	
100:5	
145:13–20	

3. We can count on God's watchful care and guidance when we walk through difficult and hazardous paths, but he may not eliminate the hardships or show us what the future holds. The deserts of life still require us to walk a difficult, uncertain path. How do the following passages help you to

better comprehend God's idea of walking on unknown paths through life's deserts with confidence and faith?

a. According to James 4:13 – 15, how much of our future do we control, and how ought we to speak about the future and God's provision for it?

b. In what ways is Paul's teaching in 2 Corinthians 5:7 similar to what God taught the Israelites as they walked through desert places where they could not see very far ahead?

c. What expectation and attitude toward God's provision does the Lord's Prayer illustrate, and how does it differ from what we often want, especially when we are fearful about the future? (See Matthew 6:9 – 13, note verse 11.)

d. In the ancient world, an oil lamp provided about as much light as a candle. So, when Psalm 119:105 portrays God's Word as a "lamp," how much of our "path" would it light at any given time? How might this image help us to adjust our desire to see everything that awaits us far down the path ahead?

4. As we go through life, where we are sure to face desert experiences, where does God want us to place our hope for the future? (See 1 Timothy 6:17; Hebrews 13:5 – 6.)

Reflection

Certainly it's wise to plan for certain situations, but God cautions us not to believe that we can provide everything for ourselves. His desire is for us to learn to be content as we rely on him to provide for us and to light our way when we face the unknown. So he led the Israelites through difficult desert paths to teach them to trust him for what the future held.

It wasn't easy. The Israelites grumbled, complained, and struggled. And so do we. Psalm 73 vividly portrays our human struggle to rely on God's faithful provision and guidance when life is difficult rather than focusing our trust and hope in whatever we can grasp for ourselves. Take some time to read this psalm, particularly verses 1 – 5 and 16 – 28.

In what ways have you struggled during difficult times, as the writer of Psalm 73 did, to draw near to God and trust him to guide your steps and provide for you?

When have you envied seemingly struggle-free people, and what did they have that led you to turn your focus away from God?

What caused you to discover the futility of trying to solve everything yourself rather than relying on God to meet your needs and be your refuge?

What do you most appreciate about relying on God's guidance and provision as you walk through the deserts of your life?

What has God been teaching you about trusting him step by step as you walk into the unknown?

After you learn something new about trusting God as you walk unknown desert paths, how long do you remember to live by what you have learned?

What attitudes, expectations, or situations tend to draw you back into self-sufficiency?

How has God's faithfulness to you during desert times given you confidence to face whatever the future holds?

Memorize

Trust in the LORD *with all your heart*
    and lean not on your own understanding;
in all your ways acknowledge him,
    and he will make your paths straight.
Do not be wise in your own eyes;

Proverbs 3:5 – 7

Day Two | Desert Life Is Hard, But God Is There

The Very Words of God

I cared for you in the desert,
    in the land of burning heat.

Hosea 13:5

Bible Discovery

When Life Gets Tough, Where Will We Turn?

The stark, rugged beauty of the deserts of the Sinai Peninsula and the Promised Land is stunning. The desert landscape is as dramatic as it is harsh and difficult, desolate and scorched. To walk into the desert for any distance is to put one's strength and endurance to the test. And for the unprepared traveler, the desert environment can lead to death.

The searing, relentless heat of the desert sun quickly saps one's energy and overwhelms the senses. It blurs one's thinking. It causes pounding headaches and lightheadedness. Water is necessary for survival, but water sources in these deserts are scarce, and rainfall is nearly nonexistent. So desert travelers must carry their own water, which quickly becomes nearly too hot to drink and provides little refreshment. Under these conditions, it is not unusual to need help desperately or to feel as if death is near.

In ancient times, God used the harsh, desert environment to test his people — to prove the character of their hearts — and see where they would place their trust when they were desperate. Although

WHERE WOULD YOU TURN FOR HELP IN THIS DESERT?

we may not walk through physical deserts, we too face times when the scorching heat of desertlike experiences beats down on us. We too come to the end of our strength and endurance. We feel exhausted, overwhelmed, indecisive, and powerless to save ourselves. The key question for us as we face our deserts is the same as it was for God's people during ancient times: Will we turn to God, who promises to meet us in our deserts, to save us from harm, and to help us to endure, or will we seek relief in some other way?

1. As you read the following Bible portions, try to imagine what it would feel like and how hard it would be to endure life in the desert.

    a. How difficult was life in the desert for Jacob, and how was he able to endure? (See Genesis 31:40 – 42.)

    b. What was desert life like for the Israelites, and how did they survive? (See Numbers 20:4 – 5; Deuteronomy 8:11, 15 – 16.)

c. What would it be like to lose your way in the desert and know that your life was slipping away if God did not help you? (See Psalms 107:4 – 9; 63:1.)

d. How do these images shape your understanding of the intensity of the struggle God's people faced to survive in the desert, and what insight do these images give you into the intensity of the struggle in your desert experiences?

POINT TO PONDER

God Shelters His People from Their Desert Enemies

In the phrase "the sun will not harm you by day" (Psalm 121:6), the Hebrew word translated "harm" can also mean "hit," "attack," or "smite." So in the minds of God's ancient people, the sun was the source of the heat that "attacks" by day and the moon was the source of cold that "attacks" at night. Therefore, they saw the pillar of cloud by day and the pillar of fire by night by which God led them in the desert as a shelter from their enemies — daytime heat and desert cold.

The concrete way God's ancient people thought about their world, their God, and their relationship with him helped to make his presence with them in the desert vivid and real. How might your perspective on your desert experiences change if you viewed the sources of your painful suffering as enemies striking against you? How might your cry to God for protection from these enemies differ from how you have asked for his help in the past and how you have expected him to respond?

2. As difficult and harmful as the desert can be, God does not abandon his people in the desert, nor does he want them to suffer harm. What does God long for his people to experience in the desert? (See Psalms 23:4; 121:5 – 8; Jeremiah 17:7 – 8; Hosea 13:4 – 5; Revelation 7:16 – 17.)

    Where is God and what is he doing when his people suffer in the desert?

    What does God long for his people to do when the heat of desert experiences saps their strength, causing them to wonder if they can continue on?

    How might this insight into God's perspective influence the way you view your desert experiences?

3. Read Psalm 78:17 – 33 and Jeremiah 17:5 – 6. According to these texts, when people reject God's provision and choose not to turn toward him when they are in need, what are the consequences?

What insight do these passages provide regarding your attitudes toward God's provision when you face desert times?

What insight do they provide regarding the significance of choosing to believe God and turn to him for help?

Reflection

When people today actually experience what it is like to walk deep into the unforgiving deserts of the Sinai Peninsula and the ancient Promised Land, their hearts often are deeply stirred as they recall how God trained and shaped his ancient people in these desert lands. As they experience the shimmering heat and difficult terrain that God's ancient people faced, it is not uncommon for them to doubt their ability to continue hiking. The experience gives them a new appreciation for the effort God's ancient people put into facing the desert's daily challenges and for the importance of what God wanted to teach his people when they reached the end of their strength and resources.

The physical challenges of the desert also speak loudly to our own times of hardship and struggle with relationships, disease, and loss. The desert — with its pain, incredible thirst, relentless sun, and overwhelming sense of not being able to take even one more step — is still a metaphor for life's hard times. A battle with cancer, the breakup of a relationship, the death of a loved one, a child who walks away from God, and many more of life's challenges hit against us and sap our strength like the suffocating heat and scorching winds of the desert. Yet the overwhelming message of the Bible is that God is in the desert too. He desires that our deserts shape us into people who trust him and faithfully turn to him for help when our path is hard and painful, when the heat of our desert leaves us exhausted and discouraged.

Think of a difficult life situation with which you struggle (or have struggled) and consider how well the desert metaphor fits that situation.

In what ways does the desert metaphor help you to describe and better understand your time of intense struggle?

What "scorching heat" did you face, and which steep, rocky obstacles blocked your path?

How did the situation drain your strength physically, emotionally, and spiritually?

When did you wonder if you could continue, or if you might die in the struggle?

During our desert experiences, we — like God's ancient people — must make the crucial choice to cling to God and his promises of provision and strength or to seek help elsewhere.

In what did you trust to keep going through your desert experiences, and where did you turn for help?

What did you realize about yourself and your trust in God and his promises during the time you struggled in your desert?

What does it mean to you that God's people who have struggled through desert experiences before you have found that God is faithful to watch over and care for his people when they seek his help?

How might what you have explored during this session influence your future response to desert situations?

Memorize

The Lord watches over you —
    the Lord is your shade at your right hand;
the sun will not harm you by day,
    nor the moon by night.
The Lord will keep you from all harm —
    he will watch over your life;
the Lord will watch over your coming and going
    both now and forevermore.

Psalm 121:5 – 8

Day Three | God Provides Shade in the Desert

The Very Words of God

> *He who dwells in the shelter of the Most High*
> *will rest in the shadow of the Almighty.*
> *I will say of the LORD, "He is my refuge and my fortress,*
> *my God, in whom I trust."*

> *Psalm 91:1 – 2*

Bible Discovery

God's Shade Is Just Enough

Shade in the desert is a great relief, particularly during the summer months when the sky often is cloudless and temperatures reach 120 degrees Fahrenheit or higher. Early in the morning and late in the day, as the sun rises and sets over the desert, the shadows of hills and mountains provide welcome relief from the intense heat. But for much of the day, the sun blazes overhead and hot winds quickly evaporate any moisture. Just standing in the intense, desert heat quickly overwhelms a person.

Shade, however, is scarce in the desert lands of the Bible (as it some-times is in the desert experiences of our lives). So desert travelers learn to appreciate even the smallest areas of shade where the temperature drops a few degrees and the wind feels just a little cooler. In the shade, one can rest for a bit before venturing into the heat again. Even the shade of a small shrub can make the difference between living or dying.

1. When Abraham sent away his son, Ishmael, and the boy's mother Hagar, they wandered in the desert near Beersheba. Locate this desert region on the map on page 59 and imagine what it would be like to go into this desert with only the food and water you could carry on your back. How long do you think a person might survive with only those provisions? (See Genesis 21:8 – 20.)

When their water ran out and death seemed imminent, where did Hagar place Ishmael?

What else did God provide in the desert to spare their lives?

FOR GREATER UNDERSTANDING
How Much Shade Did God Provide?

When we think of "shade," we may picture the broad circle of shade under a great oak tree or the deep, cool darkness under a towering evergreen. But there are no oaks or evergreens in the desert. In fact, any large trees or bushes are rare. What the Bible describes as a "bush" or "tree" in the desert near Beersheba is most likely a broom tree (Hebrew: *rotem*). Wide on top and narrow on the bottom, the broom tree is often the only shade available in the deep desert.

The white broom tree (scientific name: *Retama raetam*; translated "juniper" in the King James Version) is common in Middle Eastern deserts. Unlike many other desert shrubs, it remains green throughout the year. It normally grows in depressions or cracks in the rock where small amounts of moisture collect. It has deep roots and can absorb moisture through its leaves, so it can survive extremely harsh conditions. It grows slowly to about six feet tall and can be up to ten feet wide.

In early spring, when the broom tree is covered with myriad small, white flowers, it brings beauty to the harsh desert landscape. Its leaves grow during the rainy season and are more like pine needles than broad leaves, producing light shade that filters the sunlight just enough to make the heat tolerable.

THE SHADE OF A BROOM TREE IS JUST ENOUGH.

Fallen leaves beneath a broom tree make sitting or lying underneath more comfortable than on the hard ground. Even today, Bedouin shepherd girls will rest with their heads under the shade of a broom tree during the hottest part of the day while their flocks feed nearby.

2. In an amazing display of God's power, the prophet Elijah called down fire from heaven in order to turn the hearts of Israel back toward their God. But when evil Queen Jezebel vowed to take his life, Elijah ran into the desert near Beersheba to escape. After a day in the desert, what was Elijah's condition, and what did he do? (See 1 Kings 19:1 – 8.)

When Elijah awakened later, what else had God provided to sustain him in the desert?

What did the rest and refreshment God provided under the shade of the broom tree enable Elijah to do?

DID YOU KNOW?

The Roots of a Broom Tree

Elijah lay down under a broom tree and awakened to a fire of burning coals (1 Kings 19:3–6), a typical experience with a broom tree fire. Broom tree roots produce an exceptionally hot flame and continue to smolder as coals long after the flame is extinguished. Even today, Bedouins bake a delicious bread under a pile of charcoal from broom tree roots. Charcoal from broom tree roots is also an important trade item between Bedouins and Egyptians.

A BEDOUIN BAKES BREAD UNDER BROOM TREE COALS.

3. Isaiah 25:4 describes God as a "refuge for the poor, a refuge for the needy in his distress, a shelter from the storm and a shade from the heat." Given what you have learned about the desert lands of the Bible, how might your understanding and expectation of God's provision — "refuge," "shelter," and "shade" — differ from how people of the Bible, particularly those who lived in or near the desert, might have expected God to fulfill these descriptions?

4. Some people today equate God's protection from life's deserts as being equivalent to an air-conditioned room — perfectly controlled temperature, no glaring sun, no scorching wind, no sweat. But often God seems to provide a small amount of shade — just enough so we can continue on — rather than delivering us from the heat.

    a. When have you been suffering in one of life's deserts and experienced God's provision of a small amount of "shade"?

    b. To what extent did that shade meet your expectations or desire for help?

    c. To what extent did it meet your need by sustaining you or lightening your burden?

d.   Why do you think God provided for you as he did rather than sweeping away all of your difficulties and leaving you in the equivalent of an air-conditioned room?

e.   How did God's provision affect your ongoing journey and your relationship with him?

Reflection

Read and meditate on Psalm 121:5 – 8, which gives us a picture of God's vigilant watchfulness and faithful presence — the "shade at your right hand" — that protects us from harm as we come and go in life.

Nothing that happens in life escapes God's notice, and in the midst of our deserts — disease, loss, broken relationships, or other painful experiences — he shows up and provides just enough support and encouragement so that we can continue. Consequently, we learn to live one moment, one day, one season at a time, always seeking God for the "shade" we need today and trusting him to provide what we will need for tomorrow.

I (Ray) was blessed by my father's understanding of God's faithful provision the week after my mother died in an accident. I asked my father, "Dad, what are you doing tomorrow?" After a long pause and with a catch in his voice, he replied, "Tomorrow? Tomorrow? I cannot think about what I am going to do fifteen minutes from now let alone tomorrow. God is just enough to handle the pain right now."

What example(s) of God's faithfulness in sustaining people who are suffering in one of life's deserts provide a blessing and encouragement to you?

God's blessings often come in the form of a single broom tree situated in the middle of a rocky plateau. The desert is still daunting. Travel to the next location will be difficult. The sun remains hot, and there is not as much shade as we'd like. Yet God is the shade at our right hand. He will always provide just enough to enable us to live in our "deserts." How might this perspective on the shade God provides when we struggle in the deserts of life influence how you respond to the heat of your current or future "desert"?

How confident are you that God is never farther away from you than your outstretched hand?

How confident are you that the shade God provides will be enough to keep you going?

How do you believe you ought to pray for God's presence and protection as you face the deserts of your life?

Day Four | God Is Our Shade

The Very Words of God

> *Hear my cry, O God;*
> > *listen to my prayer.*
> *From the ends of the earth I call to you,*
> > *I call as my heart grows faint;*
> > *lead me to the rock that is higher than I.*
> *For you have been my refuge,*
> > *a strong tower against the foe.*
> *I long to dwell in your tent forever*
> > *and take refuge in the shelter of your wings.*

Psalm 61:1 – 4

Bible Discovery

Depending on God for Our Shade and Protection

We may not know or understand why we find ourselves in desert experiences, but while God doesn't promise escape from the struggle, he does promise to be with us and to help us. When the harshness of the desert threatens to overwhelm us, he is there — watching, guiding, protecting, and sustaining. As we cry out to him for help, he provides just enough shade, just enough protection, just enough guidance so that we can get around the next bend or make it through the next day. And when we cry out to him the next time, he is there again and again. His abiding love draws us to him and by his faithfulness we learn to trust him, rely on him, and love him.

1. Biblical writers often used *shade* and *shadow* to convey the images of protection and refuge that God provides. As you read the following portions of the Psalms, consider how the writer needed, longed for, and depended on God's shade and protection. Then consider how these images contribute to your understanding of what it means to depend on God in the desert, or as the Bible also says, to come out of the desert "leaning on her Beloved."

Psalm	The Writer's Understanding of Leaning on God	My Understanding of Leaning on God
17:6–8		
36:7		
57:1		
63:1, 7–8		
91:1–2		

2. Isaiah 4:2, 5–6 presents a beautiful description of the shade and protection God will provide when the promised Messiah — "the Branch of the LORD"[4] — comes and his rich blessing again rests on his people. What will the Lord himself create to be a shelter, shade, and refuge for his people gathered on Mount Zion (Jerusalem)?

   How does this picture and the promise of what God will do one day encourage you to depend on him when you face desert experiences in your life?

What are some of the ways God has been a "canopy," providing relief and shelter for you during desert experiences?

To what extent has his provision led you to trust him, lean on him, and thank him?

3. In the apostle John's vision of heaven (Revelation 7:13 – 17), he saw a great crowd of people whose days of suffering were over.

    a. Which metaphors did John use to describe what they had endured, and from what experiences did these metaphors originate? (See also Isaiah 49:10.)

    b. What is God providing for these people, and what is his relationship with them?

    c. What does this image add to your understanding of the faithful, watchful care God desires to provide for his people, and to what extent does it deepen your trust in him?

4. In what ways does the realization that the "Lamb" of Revelation 7:17 is Jesus (John 1:29), who also experienced desert times during his life on earth, give you confidence that:

    a. He joins with you and weeps with you when you experience the pain, sorrow, loneliness, and struggle of the desert?

    b. You can trust him to be your refuge and shade?[5]

Reflection

No matter which route you take, it isn't easy to walk to Jerusalem from most of the Promised Land. Many routes to Jerusalem require difficult travel through treacherous desert terrain. The road from Jericho, for example, leads through the Judea Wilderness and in places winds dangerously close to the edge of a steep canyon.

As they walked up through the desert wilderness to Jerusalem for the pilgrimage festivals, the Jewish people sang various psalms, including these words from Psalm 121:3 – 6: "He will not let your foot slip — ... the LORD watches over you — the LORD is your shade at your right hand; the sun will not harm you by day, nor the moon by night." As they walked, they kept their eyes and hearts focused on the hills ahead where the temple stood and the glory of God resided. Despite the dangers, they trusted God to watch over them so their feet would not slip. They trusted him to be their shade so the scorching heat did not overcome them.

This is the kind of trust God wants us to place in him. He leads us into desert experiences so that we might learn from him and come to know him as our shelter and shade, to love and trust him more fully, and to depend on him completely. And when God brings us out of our deserts, he desires for us to continue trusting and relying on him.

Which dangers have you faced during desert experiences?

What ability did you have to protect yourself from harm?

To what extent were you aware of God's shade — his presence and watchful care over you — and why?

What did God provide to protect and sustain you when you faced the heat of those experiences?

What thankfulness and trust has God's provision of shade during those desert experiences produced in you?

Whether you presently are walking a smooth and easy path or a treacherous and difficult one, how aware are you of God's watchful care over you?

How closely do you lean on him?

How deep and confident is your hope that you will walk in his presence forever?

Memorize

*We wait in hope for the L*ORD*;*
*   he is our help and our shield.*
In him our hearts rejoice,
*   for we trust in his holy name.*
*May your unfailing love rest upon us, O L*ORD*,*
*   even as we put our hope in you.*

Psalm 33:20 – 22

Day Five │ God Provides Shade through His People

The Very Words of God

If you do away with the yoke of oppression,
*   with the pointing finger and malicious talk,*
and if you spend yourselves in behalf of the hungry
*   and satisfy the needs of the oppressed,*
then your light will rise in the darkness,
*   and your night will become like the noonday.*
*The L*ORD *will guide you always;*
*   he will satisfy your needs in a sun-scorched land*
*   and will strengthen your frame.*
You will be like a well-watered garden,
*   like a spring whose waters never fail.*

Isaiah 58:9 – 11

Bible Discovery

God Desires His People to Be Shade in the Desert

It is amazing that the Lord God, Creator of the universe, chose to use the same flawed humans whose rebellion brought sin into his perfect creation to be his instruments in restoring *shalom* — his peace and harmony — in the world. Yet throughout human history, God has raised up and empowered such diverse people as Noah, Abraham and Sarah, Moses, Joshua, Rahab, Ruth, David, Hezekiah, Mary, and Paul to further the work of his kingdom and bring the comfort of his shade to a broken, suffering world. Today, ordinary people like you and me who follow Jesus have the opportunity to bring the refreshment of God's shade to people who suffer under the scorching heat of the "deserts" of sin and suffering.

1. Psalm 121:5-6 portrays God metaphorically as being our "shade," the one who helps and protects us. Scripture uses a number of related metaphors to help us understand what God's shade is like and the role he wants his people to play in bringing his shade, or *shalom*, to earth.

    a. The cedar tree mentioned in Ezekiel 17:22-23 is considered to be a metaphor representing the coming Messiah. What does it provide, and what is its impact on life?

    b. Which metaphor did Jesus use to describe the kingdom of heaven that he came to reveal? What does it provide, and how does it impact life? (See Mark 4:30-32.)

c. Which metaphor did the psalmist use to describe God's people, and what did God intend his people to provide when he brought them out of Egypt? (See Psalm 80:7 - 11)

2. The prophets envision a time when Israel will return to God and the Messiah will reign in righteousness and justice. What will be the role of God's people in that future kingdom? (See Isaiah 32:1 - 4; Hosea 14:1, 5 - 7.)

In what ways will each person be a channel of God's mercy during the hardships of life's deserts?

What hint of this coming kingdom was evident in the way Jesus' disciples became shade for those who were suffering shortly after Jesus ascended to heaven, and what impact do you think these actions had on those who knew the Scriptures? (See Acts 5:12 - 16.)

3. According to 2 Corinthians 1:3 - 5, what is the shade — the comfort — that God provides during our times of struggle intended to accomplish in the lives of others?

What do you think enables us to provide shade — encouragement, support, comfort — for others during their desert experiences?

What are some of the practical ways by which we can express God's shade to people who are in need? (See Matthew 25:34 - 40.)

Reflection

Remember the story of Jonah, whom God sent to Nineveh in Assyria to call its people to repentance? After his detour on a ship and inside a fish, Jonah obeyed the word of the Lord and told the Ninevites that God would destroy them because of their wickedness. But when the people repented, God spared them, which upset Jonah because he wanted the Ninevites to receive the punishment they deserved. So Jonah went out of the city to pout and see what would happen. He made a shelter to sit under and asked God to let him die.

God provided a vine to shade Jonah and to ease his discomfort, which pleased Jonah. But the next day, God sent a worm to chew through the vine. The vine withered and exposed Jonah to the scorching wind and blazing sun. As he felt the brutal heat of that desert on his head, Jonah grew faint and wanted to die. Then God said, "You have been concerned about this vine, though you did not tend it or make it grow. It sprang up overnight and died overnight. But Nineveh has more than a hundred and twenty thousand people who cannot tell their right hand from their left, and many cattle as well. Should I not be concerned about that great city?" (Jonah 4:10 - 11).

What do you think God wanted Jonah to learn about compassion, mercy, and his desire for his people to be shade to others?

What do these words cause you to realize about God's compassion, mercy, and your role in bringing his shade to people who are overwhelmed by painful desert experiences?

When has God needed to refresh your memory of the desert's harshness in order to help you remember that you are to be his shade to people who live in the desert of sin and suffering?

What shade has God provided through other people during your desert times?

How did that shade strengthen, help, and encourage you? Thank God for those people and the shade they have provided. Perhaps you might call them or send a letter of thankfulness.

How deeply do you desire God to use what you have learned in the desert to provide shade for someone else?

How might the shade you have received from God enable you to provide shade for someone else?

Memorize

Praise be to the God and Father of our Lord Jesus Christ, the Father of compassion and the God of all comfort, who comforts us in all our troubles, so that we can comfort those in any trouble with the comfort we ourselves have received from God.

2 Corinthians 1:3 – 4

HELP IS HERE

The Torah reveals that the Hebrews could have traveled from Egypt to the Promised Land in two or three weeks rather than in forty years! Yet, knowing that their journey would be painful, God had a specific purpose for leading his people into the "howling waste" of the Sinai deserts (Deuteronomy 32:10). Through hard desert experiences, God molded and shaped them to be a people prepared to enter the Promised Land, a people prepared to take their place in God's unfolding plan for redeeming his creation.

The Hebrews quickly discovered that they could not survive in the desert without God's provision. In Egypt, they had irrigated their crops during the annual Nile floods and apparently came to believe that they provided for themselves. In the Promised Land, they would depend on God's provision of annual rains that he promised would come if his people trusted him and lived by his every word. In between was the desert, where the Hebrews learned to depend on their God for everything.

Although the desert path was at times difficult and painful, God was always with his people. He led them by pillars of fire and cloud. He traveled with their camp, his presence living on the holy ark that was carried in front of the people. He faithfully provided just enough to sustain them each day.

Sometimes God's provision came suddenly and miraculously. Manna fell from the sky, water gushed from solid rock, and bitter water became fresh. The former Hebrew slaves, unskilled in warfare, defeated powerful enemies. Those who were bitten by poisonous snakes were restored to health.

At other times, God met their needs through resources he had already provided in the desert. After they experienced great thirst, God led them to the twelve wells and seventy palm trees at Elim. At the right moment, he drove migrating quail into Israel's camp in the Sinai, providing his people with meat. When they needed gold and silver, wood, and skilled craftsmen to build the tabernacle, Egypt had provided the gold and silver, the desert provided the wood, and trained craftsmen among the Hebrews completed the work.

Although it may be tempting for us to believe that God never intends for us to suffer or to face hard times, and that he prefers for us to be blessed with abundance and to never experience lack, God often leads his people into or at least allows us to experience the pain and hardships of the desert. There we learn to trust in God's presence and provision and grow into a closer, more intimate relationship with him.

The day will come when we will no longer face the exhausting heat, brutal hardships, and overwhelming thirst of our earthly deserts. Today, however, we must journey through them. We must feel the pain, the loss, the confusion, the helplessness. But God never leaves us alone or uncared for in our deserts. As he has always done for his people, he walks with us in our deserts. He faithfully provides — sometimes in dramatic, unpredictable, amazing ways — exactly what we need to take our next step.

Opening Thoughts (3 minutes)

The Very Words of God

> *This is what the LORD says:*
> *"Cursed is the one who trusts in man,*
> *who depends on flesh for his strength*
> *and whose heart turns away from the LORD.*
> *He will be like a bush in the wastelands;*
> *he will not see prosperity when it comes.*
> *He will dwell in the parched places of the desert,*
> *in a salt land where no one lives.*

> *"But blessed is the man who trusts in the* Lord,
>   *whose confidence is in him.*
> *He will be like a tree planted by the water*
>   *that sends out its roots by the stream.*
> *It does not fear when heat comes;*
>   *its leaves are always green.*
> *It has no worries in a year of drought*
>   *and never fails to bear fruit."*

Jeremiah 17:5 – 8

Think About It

When we find ourselves in a painful desert experience — financial crisis, broken relationship, illness or injury, or a time when our path demands more than we are able to give — we reach a point where our own resources fail and we lack what we need to keep going. In such situations, as in the rest of our lives, God promises to provide for those who depend on him.

In what ways has God provided for you during your desert experiences? When has he suddenly done something miraculous, or when has he provided through something that was already in place on your desert path?

How have you learned to recognize and appropriate God's provision for you?

DVD Notes (31 minutes)

God provides in the desert

The many blessings of the acacia tree

Becoming like a tree planted by streams of water

The tamarisk tree—promise of shade for future generations

The empty fruit of the *ar' ar* tree

DVD Discussion (6 minutes)

1. On the map of the Sinai Peninsula below, locate Wadi Nasb (where this session was filmed), Desert of Sin, Jebel Musa (the traditional Mount Sinai), Desert of Paran, and the Judea Wilderness.

    Except for an occasional oasis that may support a few palm trees, the trees that grow in this vast desert region are the broom tree, the acacia, the tamarisk, and the *ar' ar* (Hebrew). These trees usually appear as single trees, or occasionally in a small cluster. How does this help you

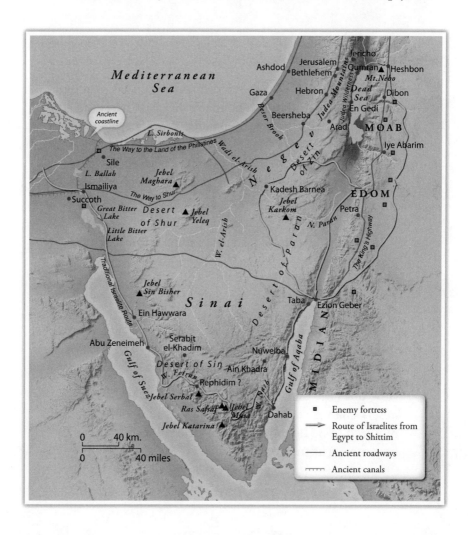

to understand why the Bedouin who live in these desert regions call the acacia tree their best friend?

2. When you realize that it may take decades, or even hundreds of years for a tree to grow to maturity in the desert, what insight do you gain into how God cares for his people as demonstrated by his provision of trees long before his people need them?

3. What insights have you gained regarding God's provision for his people in light of the many different ways the acacia tree supports life in the desert where there are few other resources?

4. What was your mental picture of what a tree planted by streams of water looked like, and how has this video changed your perception?

    How does the image of a tree planted by a stream in the *desert* change your understanding of the persistent effort required to be deeply rooted in God's words in order to become a fruitful tree?

5. When Abraham planted a tamarisk tree near Beersheba, he was making a powerful statement of his faith in God and his promises. How often do we even think of taking a step of faith that will bear fruit generations after we are gone, and how might thinking in this way change how we walk with God and experience him in our deserts?

Small Group Bible Discovery and Discussion (15 minutes)

God Has Already Provided

Abraham, a nomadic shepherd whom God chose to be the father of many nations, the father of Israel (Genesis 17:4, 20), experienced God's provision in many ways. During the years Abraham walked with God, God had provided food during times of famine, protection from angry kings, great flocks and wealth, protection for his nephew Lot, and the miraculous provision of an heir long after normal childbearing years. Abraham knew that God would provide.

After living in Egypt for hundreds of years, Abraham's descendants, the Israelites, apparently had lost sight of God's faithful provision. Then God acted mightily to deliver his people from slavery in Egypt. He led them into the desert where they began to learn, as their father Abraham had, that their God would be faithful to walk with them and provide for them, even in the desert.

1. After finally providing the son he had promised to his faithful servant Abraham, God told Abraham to sacrifice his only son, Isaac, to him. (See Genesis 22:1 – 14.)

   a. In what sense was this a desert experience for Abraham, and in what sense was it not?

   b. What did Abraham trust God to provide in the desert? What kind of faith did it take for Abraham to hope and believe in God's future provision?

   c. How did God provide what Abraham needed?

   d. What was Abraham's lasting testimony of what God had done for him on that mountain? (See v. 14.)

2. When God led his people out of Egypt and into the unforgiving deserts of the Sinai Peninsula, what had he already provided for them that would help them to survive their desert journey? (See Exodus 15:27; Numbers 11:31–32; Deuteronomy 8:4.)

3. After meeting with his people at Mount Sinai and establishing a covenant with them, God commanded them to build a sanctuary in which his presence would live among them. One might not expect that the Israelites, who left Egypt in a hurry, would have the resources they needed to

complete the job. How had God already provided exactly what his people needed to obey his commands? (See Exodus 3:21 - 22; 31:1 - 11; 35:4 - 10, 20 - 29; 36:2 - 7; 37:1.)

Faith Lesson (4 minutes)

In many ways, our seasons of pain, struggle, and suffering — our deserts — are similar to the deserts the Israelites faced. They lived in the scorching heat of difficult circumstances, thirsted for a vibrant relationship with God, didn't know where their future would lead, became discouraged, and had to choose whether or not to trust God to provide for them.

Just as God heard the cries of his ancient people, he still hears his people cry out during times of crisis — sickness, job loss, broken relationships, pain, loneliness, emptiness. Sometimes he comes alongside us providing comfort, restoration, and healing that enables us to continue walking in the desert. His provision may come in many ways — through a caring friend, an unexpected gift, a surgeon's skilled hands, or a portion of his Word, the Bible. Sometimes he miraculously takes us out of the desert.

No matter how he provides, God will meet our needs as he has promised. What is most important, however, is that we recognize God — not ourselves — as our provider. This is the life-changing truth that Abraham and his descendants, the Israelites, discovered through their desert walk with God so many years ago.

1. Our times in the desert often lead us into a deeper relationship with God as we learn to love, trust, and obey him. In what way(s) has God's provision during desert times not only provided for your survival but provided a way for you to walk more intimately with him?

2. When God uses everyday means to meet your needs in the desert, to what extent do you tend to minimize his role and take credit for what he alone has provided?

3. When you find yourself in a desert experience, in what ways are you tempted to think that you can provide for yourself rather than recognizing and being grateful for God's daily provision for you?

    What specific things will you do, starting today, to cultivate an awareness of — and thankfulness for — God's daily provision?

4. After God provided the ram for Abraham's sacrifice (Genesis 22:13 – 14), what was Abraham's testimony to what God had done for him?

    Do you think Abraham's faith in God deepened that day? If so, how?

What is your testimony of what God has provided for you? How emphatically have you declared it so that other people know what he has done for you?

Closing (1 minute)

Read aloud Genesis 22:13 – 14: "Abraham looked up and there in a thicket he saw a ram caught by its horns. He went over and took the ram and sacrificed it as a burnt offering instead of his son. So Abraham called that place The LORD Will Provide. And to this day it is said, 'On the mountain of the LORD it will be provided.' "

Then pray together, asking God to help you to trust him to meet your needs during your desert times. Ask him to help you to humbly recognize his provision for your life.

Memorize

> *Abraham looked up and there in a thicket he saw a ram caught by its horns. He went over and took the ram and sacrificed it as a burnt offering instead of his son. So Abraham called that place The* LORD *Will Provide. And to this day it is said, "On the mountain of the* LORD *it will be provided."*
>
> **Genesis 22:13 – 14**

Walking with God through Our Deserts

In-Depth Personal Study Sessions

Day One | Desert Trees: Symbols of God's Presence

The Very Words of God

> *The righteous will flourish like a palm tree,*
> > *they will grow like a cedar of Lebanon;*
> *planted in the house of the LORD,*
> > *they will flourish in the courts of our God.*
> *They will still bear fruit in old age,*
> > *they will stay fresh and green,*
> *proclaiming, "The LORD is upright;*
> > *he is my Rock, and there is no wickedness in him."*
>
> > **Psalm 92:12 – 15**

Bible Discovery

Desert Trees in God's Unfolding Story

In desert regions, particularly the most arid places such as the deserts of the Sinai Peninsula and the Judea Wilderness, trees are scarce and highly valued. When asked about specific kinds of trees, Bedouin who live in these deserts know where *every* tree in their respective territories is located! The Bible frequently mentions trees — the planting of trees, people sitting under trees, being buried under a tree, or metaphors of trees. And in Jewish tradition, the presence of trees in the desert was taken to be a sign of God's presence and provision. So for God's ancient people, desert trees were not just "accidents" of nature but were God's specific provision and a testimony to his presence. So consider the role trees in the desert play in God's unfolding plan to redeem his creation.

1. In what ways have trees represented God's presence and provision, even in hostile desert environments? (See Exodus 15:27; Leviticus 23:39 – 43; Isaiah 41:17 – 20.)

2. What is the role or symbolism of the trees mentioned in the following Bible stories? (See Genesis 12:6 – 7; 18:1 – 8; Joshua 19:31 – 33; Judges 9:7 – 15; 1 Samuel 22:6; 31:11 – 13; 1 Kings 4:20 – 25; Nehemiah 10:34 – 35.)

3. Biblical writers often used trees as metaphors for one's relationship with God. On the following chart, write down the tree metaphor and what it represents.

Text	Trees as Metaphors
Ps. 1:1 – 3	
Ps. 52:8 – 9	
Ps. 92:12	
Jer. 17:6 – 8	
Matt. 7:15 – 20	
Luke 3:7 – 9	
Rom. 11:16 – 24	

4. The image of a "tree" occurs in God's unfolding story of
    redemption from the Tree of Life in the garden of Eden to
    the Tree of Life in the age to come. In the garden of Eden,
    our ancestors opposed God's desire, ate from the Tree of
    Knowledge, and were barred from the Tree of Life. In the
    New Jerusalem, God's people again will have access to the
    Tree of Life, and its leaves will heal the nations. As you read
    the following Bible verses, take note of the role these trees
    play in God's plan to restore *shalom* to his creation.

    a. What is the significance of the two trees in the garden of
        Eden? (See Genesis 2:8 - 9, 15 - 17; 3:1 - 24.)

    b. What "tree" in the tabernacle may have reminded the
        Hebrews of the Tree of Life and God's presence with
        them? (See Exodus 25:31 - 40.)

    c. How is God restoring access to the Tree of Life for
        his people? (See Proverbs 3:13 - 18; 11:30; Matthew
        13:31 - 32; Revelation 2:7.)

    d. In what way has God used a "tree" as a Tree of Life in
        restoring humanity's relationship with God? (See Deuter-
        onomy 21:22 - 23; Acts 5:30; 10:37 - 40; 1 Peter 2:24.)

e. Where will people have full access to the Tree of Life?
(See Ezekiel 47:1 – 2, 12; Revelation 22:1 – 4.)

Reflection

We can only imagine the joy the ancient Hebrews experienced as
they walked through harsh desert terrain and saw, in the distance,
a large tree or an oasis with a number of trees. Perhaps they would
find water there or could rest under the shade. No doubt the few
desert trees they saw on their journey through the desert reminded
them of God's ongoing presence and provision.

What are the rare but refreshing provisions God has placed on
your desert path that stand out to you like trees in the desert?

How have these refreshed, strengthened, or encouraged you so
that you could continue on your journey?

What do you feel when you see another such "tree" ahead of you
as you walk your desert path?

Prayerfully consider the ways in which you may be like the following desert trees (see page 116), and ask God to show you
what he desires you to learn from each:

Ar' ar. If we depend on our own strength, we may look beautiful and successful, but our fruit will be dry and empty, filled only with the dust of death. The *ar' ar* uses precious water for itself but produces nothing of value.

Acacia. God has prepared acacia trees to handle the heat and drought of difficult times. He will enable us to do the same if our roots sink deeply into God and his Word. In order to become God's provision for other desert travelers, we must be willing to live in the desert.

Tamarisk. The slow-growing tamarisk must be cultivated and represents the future. God desires for us to fully trust him and depend on his provision in the desert — not just for ourselves, but for those who come after us.

Memorize

I am like an olive tree
*   flourishing in the house of God;*
I trust in God's unfailing love
*   for ever and ever.*
I will praise you forever for what you have done;
*   in your name I will hope, for your name is good.*
*   I will praise you in the presence of your saints.*

Psalm 52:8 – 9

Day Two | The Curse of Trusting in Ourselves

The Very Words of God

> *This is what the Lord says:*
> *"Cursed is the one who trusts in man,*
>   *who depends on flesh for his strength*
>   *and whose heart turns away from the Lord.*
> *He will be like a bush in the wastelands;*
>   *he will not see prosperity when it comes.*
> *He will dwell in the parched places of the desert,*
>   *in a salt land where no one lives."*
>
>   **Jeremiah 17:5 – 6**

Bible Discovery

The Ar' ar Tree: Accursed Symbol of Self-Sufficiency

"Cursed is the one who trusts in man ... depends on flesh ... whose heart turns away from the Lord." When Jeremiah pronounced these powerful words, God's people not only had worshiped other gods but had become convinced that their success was due to their own efforts, not God's provision. They were at risk of receiving God's judgment for their unfaithfulness.

To ensure that God's people understood the gravity of their unfaithfulness, Jeremiah compared them to a desert "bush" — a word that some leading scholars link to the tree called "Sodom Apple" (*ar' ar* in Hebrew), which is an apt illustration of self-sufficient people who do not depend on God. Jeremiah added impact to his message by using *arur*, the Hebrew word translated "cursed" and nearly the same Hebrew word as *ar' ar*, that is translated "bush." This clever wordplay subtly strengthened the connection between "cursed" and "bush." What could have compelled Jeremiah to deliver such a strong message?

    1.   What had taken place in the hearts of God's people that kindled God's anger? (See Jeremiah 17:1 – 4.)

2. Read Jeremiah 17:5–8, and notice the two perspectives from which we can live life. Then contrast the path God's people had apparently taken with the path God desired them to walk.

	Cursed is the one who trusts in man ...	Blessed is the man who trusts in the LORD ...
What impact does each choice have on a person's relationship with God?		
What does each person become like?		
In what kind of place does each person grow?		
What are each person's worries about the future?		

DID YOU KNOW?

Jeremiah Knew His Trees

Jeremiah lived in Anathoth (Jeremiah 1:1), where the Wilderness of Judea meets the more fertile Judea Mountains. God sent him to Perath (Jeremiah 13:1–7), which is believed to be an oasis named Ein Perath or the Spring of Perath located a short distance into that desert. Many acacia trees grow in the desert canyons east of Perath, and many *ar' ar* trees grow by the Spring of Perath. So, Jeremiah was clearly familiar with both kinds of trees.

3. According to Deuteronomy 8:2 – 5 and Hosea 2:8 – 15, why did God bring his people into the desert, and why would he — either figuratively or physically — lead them back there later?

What do you think of the irony of someone being like a self-reliant bush in the desert — the very place God uses to teach his people to trust and depend on him?

When you find yourself in a desert experience, how important would it be for you to discover why God brought you to that place?

DATA FILE

The Ar' ar (Sodom Apple) Tree

Believed to be the cursed tree about which Jeremiah wrote, the *ar' ar* tree grows in severe Middle Eastern deserts where it may be the only living tree in sight. In the summer and fall, abundant green fruit the size of a large apple grows in clusters of three to four. The fruit appears to be exactly what hungry and thirsty desert travelers desire — full, moist, sweet. However, when the fruit is broken open it is dry and empty except for a hard pit, fine dust, long fibrous strands, and droplets of toxic white juice.

continued on next page . . .

THE *AR' AR* TREE IS STUNNINGLY BEAUTIFUL, BUT ITS "FRUIT" IS WORTHLESS FOR FOOD.

It is believed that this tree was named Sodom Apple because it looks fertile but has no nutritional value and is, in fact, filled with death. It is a reminder of the attractive city of Sodom that to Abraham's nephew, Lot, seemed full of opportunity. But as Lot discovered, Sodom was full of deadly evil and God destroyed it (Genesis 13:5 – 12; 18:16 – 33; 19:1 – 25).

Reflection

The *ar' ar* tree, like the acacia, is well suited for surviving extreme desert conditions. It has deep roots, goes dormant when it has insufficient water, and springs to life again when the rains come. It produces beautiful flowers and lovely fruit, but unlike the acacia its fruit is merely an empty shell that can't nourish anything. So when Jeremiah compared people who trust in themselves rather than in God to the *ar' ar* tree, it was a strong condemnation.

To some extent, we all want to look great and appear successful, but that can be hard to do especially when we ourselves are in the desert and are needy. How important is it for you to trust in

God to provide what you need in the desert rather than to pursue your own solution and enslave yourself to gods of your own making?

What is it about yourself that you tend to trust, especially when the path before you is difficult and uncertain? Is it your abilities? Intelligence? Charisma?

How do you find a balance between using your God-given talents and resources while maintaining a heart that is completely submissive and dependent on his provision?

According to the Word of the Lord, one consequence of trusting in ourselves is that we "will not see prosperity when it comes." When we assume responsibility for meeting our own needs, life becomes a stressful, worrisome struggle to provide what we need and want — not just for today, but for tomorrow and the next day as well. Providing for ourselves becomes, in a sense, its own desert. When have you stepped into the desert of trying to meet your own needs?

During that time, to what extent did your efforts create worry and stress?

During that time, what happened to your ability to appreciate and enjoy what God had already provided for you?

In contrast, how does living in a trusting dependence on God relieve you of worry and stress, and make you more aware of and grateful for his provision?

Memorize

*Who among you fears the L*ORD
   and obeys the word of his servant?
Let him who walks in the dark,
   who has no light,
*trust in the name of the L*ORD
   and rely on his God.
But now, all you who light fires
   and provide yourselves with flaming torches,
go, walk in the light of your fires
   and of the torches you have set ablaze.
This is what you shall receive from my hand:
   You will lie down in torment.

Isaiah 50:10–11

Day Three | The Acacia Tree:
A Symbol of God's Provision

The Very Words of God

The poor and needy search for water,
　but there is none;
　their tongues are parched with thirst.
But I the Lord *will answer them;*
　I, the God of Israel, will not forsake them....
I will put in the desert
　the cedar and the acacia, the myrtle and the olive.
I will set pines in the wasteland,
　the fir and the cypress together,
so that people may see and know,
　may consider and understand,
that the hand of the Lord *has done this,*
　that the Holy One of Israel has created it.

Isaiah 41:17, 19 – 20

Bible Discovery

God Provides Everything We Need — in the Desert and Where We Have Plenty

Acacia trees grow along the edges of wadis, barren riverbeds in harsh deserts that may receive water a few times a year or only a few times in a decade or more! If conditions are too dry, acacia trees become dormant and come alive again when floodwaters pass through. Their leaves appear first, then small flowers, followed by fruit pods.

These amazing trees are a testimony to God's ever-present provision in the desert. They provide life-saving shade as well as firewood, sap used for medicinal and other purposes, and fodder for camels and goats. No wonder these treasured trees are called "the Bedouin's best friend."

As we walk through our deserts, God sometimes takes us out of the heat and hardship and leads us into a more pleasant place as he

**IN THIS WADI, FLOODWATERS SPREAD OUT OVER A WIDE AREA, ALLOW-
ING ACACIA TREES TO GROW ALONG THE EDGE OF THE RIVERBED.**

did when he guided the new generation of Israelites into the Promised Land. At other times, he walks with us on the desert path and
guides us step by step to the "acacia trees" of our deserts. Often we
find that his provision has been firmly rooted in the desert for many
years and provides just enough shade and rest to sustain us on our
desert path.

1. Carefully read Isaiah 41:17 – 20. What did God promise to do
    for his thirsty people in the desert, and in what way(s) had
    he already provided for their needs?

    For what reason (in addition to his compassion and loving
    care) did God do this for his people?

As you remember the desert experiences of your life, what have you come to know and understand through God's provision for you?

DATA FILE
The Acacia Tree

The acacia tree with its often slanted, flat top is conspicuous in the desert landscape. It is native to Middle Eastern deserts and its gnarled, twisted, windblown look matches its desert life. When infrequent floods wash through the wadis where the acacia grows, it erupts into globular, densely clustered, white or yellow flowers. Later it produces small, brown, twisted fruit pods containing several hard seeds. These are used for animal feed, and the Bedouin say one kilo of seed pods will provide a week's fodder for a camel.

THE DELICATE FLOWERS OF THE ACACIA TREE

The thorn-covered branches of the acacia have small, compound leaves that help to conserve water, but during times of drought the tree can drop all of its leaves and become dormant. Despite this resiliency, the tree is sensitive to any changes in its water intake. Even the tread marks of a four-wheel-drive vehicle can kill a nearby acacia tree.

Because the acacia tree grows so slowly, its wood is hard, dense, and difficult for water to penetrate. The heartwood is dark red/orange brown and contains substances that make it resistant to decay and unattractive to

continued on next page . . .

THIS SMALL ACACIA LIMB, ABOUT 2.5 INCHES IN DIAMETER, IS MORE THAN ONE HUNDRED YEARS OLD. NOTICE ITS SMALL GROWTH RINGS AND THE THORNS THAT KEEP ANIMALS OTHER THAN CAMELS AND GOATS FROM EATING ITS LEAVES.

insects. Acacia wood is used for cabinetmaking, and its bark is used in tanning leather. It also produces fibers for making rope and sap (gum Arabic) that is used as medicine and in food products. When a tree dies, its roots, branches, and trunk make excellent charcoal and long-burning (twenty-four-hour) logs for cooking fires.

2. When God commanded his people to build the tabernacle in the desert, which kind of wood did he instruct them to use to build the structure and to make certain of its furnishings? (See Exodus 25:1 – 30; 26:15 – 32, 36 – 37; 27:1 – 8.)

Why do you think God chose this wood — commonly found in the desert — for building the tabernacle?

In what way(s) might this illustrate how God uses common things of the desert to bless his people?

DATA FILE
The Ark of the Covenant

God carefully instructed Moses how the Israelites were to build the ark of the covenant—the most sacred object to be kept in the Holy of Holies in the tabernacle. Built of acacia wood, the ark was an oblong chest, 2.5 cubits (3.75 feet) long and 1.5 cubits (2.25 feet) high and wide. It was covered inside and out with pure gold and had a gold molding around its sides with rings on the four corners of the short sides for carrying poles. It was carried in front of the people so that it faced the direction in which they were walking.

On the ark rested a slab of gold 2.5 by 1.5 cubits (3.75 by 2.25 feet) called the "atonement cover." Rising out of this golden cover two cherubim, one from each end, faced the center with their wings extended over the cover. Inside, the ark contained the tablets of the Ten Words (Ten Commandments) documenting the covenant God made with the Hebrews at Mount Sinai. The ark remained in the Holy of Holies except when it was being transported during the Israelites' desert travels. Its poles were never to be removed and later remained in the temple Solomon built in Jerusalem (1 Kings 8:8).

It is fitting that acacia trees, a symbol of God's presence and blessing in the desert, were used to build the ark of the covenant and the tabernacle. God's people desperately needed his presence with them, so he chose a dwelling constructed of material that he had already provided for his people in the desert. Then he came and lived among them, spoke with them, healed and guided them, and forgave them. Imagine how this must have encouraged them. Their God was with them during their hard desert journey!

3. What warning did God give his people as they prepared to leave behind the hardships of the desert, where he had provided everything they needed, and to enter the Promised Land? (See Deuteronomy 6:10 – 12.)

What had God already prepared the land to provide for his people in the Promised Land?

What might his people forget when they had what they needed in abundance?

Reflection

We can derive hope from the wonderful truth that God not only provided the acacia wood necessary for the Israelites' survival and the building of the tabernacle, but nurtured those acacia trees in the desert for centuries so that they would be exactly where they were needed! That is one of the miraculous ways he provides for us during our desert times.

After my heart attack and bypass surgery a few years ago, I (Ray) realized that I might not live long unless I adopted a different, healthier diet. Soon I discovered that my wife, Esther, had always wanted to move toward a healthier diet. I had not expected God to provide for me in this way, but Esther was already prepared — like an acacia tree in the desert — to provide what God knew I would need.

God often provides modern-day equivalents of acacia trees that not only meet our needs but help us to experience his loving presence during our most painful deserts. When have you discovered that God in some way already had provided for you by using something or someone within your desert to provide for your needs?

Did he meet your needs through another person or insights gained from an earlier experience? Did he use a book you had read or studied — maybe a Bible passage you memorized?

To what extent did you recognize his hand at work in your life at that time?

How does God's provision of "acacia trees" help you to recognize his loving and faithful presence in the deserts of your life?

God's provision is never far away. If you are struggling through a difficult desert experience, will you turn to him, recognize his providence ... and thankfully receive what he will provide for you?

Memorize

I will put in the desert
  the cedar and the acacia, the myrtle and the olive.
I will set pines in the wasteland,
  the fir and the cypress together,
so that people may see and know,
  may consider and understand,
that the hand of the LORD has done this,
  that the Holy One of Israel has created it.

Isaiah 41:19 – 20

POINT TO PONDER

God Desires ... and Empowers ... Our Best Efforts

The ark of the covenant was built of dense, heavy acacia wood covered with gold. It supported the atonement cover and held the heavy stone tablets of the Ten Words (Ten Commandments). Obviously the ark was quite heavy, and when the Israelites moved camp four Levites carried it using gold-covered acacia wood poles.

Although the Hebrew Bible does not reveal the ark's weight, some scholars estimate it at more than two thousand pounds! This raises some questions. How could four Levite men carry such a heavy object? How could the rings, attached to a thin covering of gold on the acacia-wood box, hold such weight when the poles were inserted? How could the poles support such weight? No one knows these answers for certain, but Jewish tradition has an answer: "We [Hebrews] did not carry the ark, the ark carried us."

This perspective offers an important lesson for those of us who walk in difficult deserts. After God delivered his people from Egypt, he gave them a specific and difficult task: to walk through the desert to Mount Sinai. They arrived at their destination, but not because of their own strength. God had carried them "on eagles' wings" (Exodus 19:4), meaning that his power working in and through them had made their journey successful.

The same is likely true of the heavy ark. God commanded the Levites to carry it, and after they made a great effort to lift it, they were able to carry it all the way to the Promised Land! God's power working through them made it possible.

This same principle is evident in our walk with God. God asks us to expend every ounce of effort to follow (obey) him and remain on his path. Yet it is through his strength and his Spirit that we are empowered to accomplish this. For example, God commanded, "Be holy, because I am holy" (Leviticus 11:45), yet he is the one who makes us holy (Exodus 31:13). Jesus commanded those of us who follow him to demonstrate our love for him by obeying his commands, yet he also said, "Apart from me you can do nothing" (John 15:5). In the same vein, Paul wrote that "the weakness of God is stronger than man's strength" (1 Corinthians 1:25). The key is to give God our maximum effort, yet realize that our accomplishments are made possible by God's mighty work within us.

When have you expended great effort to faithfully follow God? Did you succeed? Whose strength enabled you to accomplish the task? Would you have been successful if you had not expended significant effort? And yet ... how much of it did God accomplish?

Day Four | A Tree Planted by the Water

The Very Words of God

> Blessed is the man who trusts in the L{\scriptsize ORD},
>   whose confidence is in him.
> He will be like a tree planted by the water
>   that sends out its roots by the stream.
> It does not fear when heat comes;
>   its leaves are always green.
> It has no worries in a year of drought
>   and never fails to bear fruit.
>
> *Jeremiah 17:7 – 8*

Bible Discovery

To Be Like an Acacia Tree

The acacia tree grows in the harshest deserts, where it benefits those who struggle to survive. For a desert traveler, one acacia can make the difference between life and death. But what enables acacia trees to survive in the desert for literally hundreds of years, even during years of terrible drought?

The answer lies in their roots. Acacia roots grow deep under the wadis where floodwaters occasionally pass in order to draw water from underground long after the floods have dried up. Large, strong roots firmly anchor these trees so that they can survive the rushing waters of severe floods that can be more than ten feet deep. So if God's people who trust in him are to be like the acacia tree that is planted by streams of water, where are we to put down our roots?

THE SHADE OF THE ACACIA TREE PROVIDES JUST ENOUGH RELIEF FROM THE SCORCHING HEAT OF THE DESERT SUN. ROOTS GROW DEEP UNDERGROUND TO FIRMLY ANCHOR THE ACACIA TREE IN THE WADI.

1. Jeremiah 17:7 – 8 compares people who trust in God to the acacia tree, the tree planted by the stream of water in the desert. In what ways are God's people to be like these trees?

    What would you say is the "fruit" that God's people are to provide in the desert?

    How does placing our trust and confidence in God enable us to avoid being overwhelmed by the fear of "heat" and "drought" that are part of desert life?

    What would you say enables God's people to bear fruit even when they are facing their own desert struggles and suffering?

2. The acacia survives because its roots sink deeply into the wadi where it finds life-giving water. As God's people who are part of his provision for others in the desert, we survive by sinking our roots deeply into the living water of God's presence, his Word, and his people. What do the following

portions of the Bible reveal about growing strong, life-sustaining roots?

Text	Growing Strong, Life-Sustaining Roots
Pss. 9:10; 20:7; Prov. 3:5–8	
Deut. 10:12–13; Matt. 22:37–38	
Pss. 5:3; 69:13	
1 Thess. 5:16–18	
Pss. 1:1–3; 112:1; 119:33–40	

Reflection

Even during our desert times, we can be planted by the streams of living water of God's presence, his Word, and his people. If our roots sink deeply into him, we have no need to fear desert heat and drought. We may experience painful, barren times, but as God provides we will never fail to bear fruit that will benefit others in their life's deserts.

Following my (Ray's) heart surgery, God provided significant blessings through several "acacia tree" people who had had the same procedure as I had. Some of them were still suffering, but they spent time with me — encouraging me, praying with me, motivating me, and loving me. I desperately needed their fruit, which God used to sustain me in my desert.

Being like trees planted by streams may require us to deliberately live in the desert with other suffering people so that we can provide for them and help them to be fruitful. The question is, are we willing to be in the desert in order to bear fruit that benefits others in the desert? Jesus was. He left heaven for the desert of suffering, rejection, and death in order to bear the fruit that gives me life. He joins me in my desert, bearing fruit like an acacia. As his disciple, I desire to follow his example.

How deep are your spiritual "roots" right now, and what is the relationship between your ability to draw nourishment from God, his Word, and his people and your ability to withstand the heat and drought of the desert?

When life is difficult and painful — like an acacia tree growing in a dry wadi during an extended drought — how will you continue to "bear fruit" for God?

What has God been teaching you recently about trusting him more completely and sinking your roots deeper into his Word?

Think about someone who has been like a fruitful acacia tree for you during overwhelming desert struggles. How did this person strengthen and encourage you, and what did you learn from him or her about trusting God during desert times?

How might you be such a tree to other people who struggle in the desert?

THINK ABOUT IT
Feed on God's Word

To be like an acacia tree in the desert, or to plant and keep alive a tamarisk tree, requires great faith and a commitment to ongoing effort. It requires that we know God intimately, trust him completely, and obey him faithfully. As the Israelites learned through their desert journey, we do this by learning to live by every word from the mouth of God. This is why, after Moses died, God said to Joshua, "Do not let this Book of the Law depart from your mouth; meditate on it day and night, so that you may be careful to do everything written in it" (Joshua 1:8).

To Westerners, meditating on God's Word is often viewed as a passive, quiet practice. But to the Hebrew mind, meditation is that and much more. The word translated "meditate" in Joshua 1:8 (Hebrew: *ha'gah*) is the same word translated "growls" in Isaiah 31:4, which describes God's fury against those who would destroy his people. *Ha'gah* conveys the fierce intensity of a hungry lion after a kill.

For us then, *ha'gah* conveys the picture of an intense commitment to tear into God's every word, devour every morsel, savor its taste, and long for more. The one who meditates intensely "eats" the text[1] like someone who has received fresh bread from heaven! Then the Word of God becomes a part of us and works within us so that we become the people who can stand like acacia trees in the desert and be God's provision for other desert travelers. May each of us take to heart God's words to Joshua.

Day Five | The Tamarisk Tree: a Testimony to the Future

The Very Words of God

> *Abraham planted a tamarisk tree in Beersheba, and there he called upon the name of the LORD, the Eternal God.*
>
> **Genesis 21:33**

Bible Discovery

Abraham Planted a Tamarisk Tree

At first glance, the phrase "Abraham planted a tamarisk tree" probably seems insignificant. After all, people have planted trees for thousands of years. In the big picture, what difference will one tree make at the edge of the Negev desert? By planting that tree then and there, Abraham was making a tremendous statement of faith in God — not unlike building an altar or setting up standing stones as a memorial to what God had done.

1. God called Abraham to leave his homeland and his people and go to a land that he would show him. What did God promise to do if Abraham obeyed God's command? (See Genesis 12:1 – 7.)

   What further promises did God make to Abraham regarding his descendants and the land he would give to him? (See Genesis 13:14 – 18.)

What did God do to confirm that he would make his promises come true? (See Genesis 15:4 – 19; 17:1 – 8.)

When Abraham died, how much of the promised land did he actually own? (See Genesis 25:7 – 11.)

Why do you think Abraham continued to believe God's promises even though he did not see them fulfilled during his lifetime?

2. Even though Abraham lived in the land of Canaan, he owned very little of it. Who claimed the land promised to Abraham, and what did Abraham do to live peacefully in that land? (See Genesis 21:22 – 32.)

3. After the conflict between Abraham and Abimelech was resolved, what did Abraham do? (See Genesis 21:33.)

What did the act of planting a tamarisk tree at Beersheba affirm — about his future family, his faith and trust in God, and his commitment to future generations of his descendants?

DATA FILE
The Tamarisk Tree

The shade of a tall, slow-growing tamarisk (salt cedar) tree is a blessing in the desert. It usually grows in sandy soils with a higher saline content, and is one of few trees found on the shores of the Dead Sea. It can grow as high as forty to sixty feet.

The small, feathery leaves of the tamarisk excrete salt crystals that the tree absorbs from the soil through small glands on its long tap roots. The encrusted salt on the leaves, in turn, absorbs the little moisture in the air. As the salty

THIS TALL, SLOW-GROWING TAMARISK PROVIDES COOLING SHADE IN THE DESERT.

continued on next page . . .

water droplets evaporate from the leaves in the heat, the air beneath the tree is cooled. No wonder desert travelers and shepherds prize this tree.

The tamarisk, however, grows very slowly and requires much more water than other desert trees. Seedlings require extended periods of soil saturation in order to thrive, so this tree rarely grows on its own. It must be cared for and cultivated, but the person who plants it will not live to enjoy its cooling shade. To meet the tree's need for water, Bedouin often plant tamarisk trees in wadis where floodwater collects or can be trapped to saturate the ground and allow the tree to grow. As one elderly Bedouin man explained, "We plant tamarisks for our grandchildren," apparently meaning, "Because they grow so slowly and last for a long time, we will not enjoy them but our grandchildren will."

Reflection

Although modern culture stresses living for ourselves and expending every effort to obtain the enjoyment we desire, those of us who are Christ followers have a greater purpose in life. God is reclaiming his world, bringing *shalom* through us. He desires for us to stand on the shoulders of those godly people who came before us and to fulfill faithfully our part in God's unfolding story by preparing the way for those who will come after us. Just as a planted tamarisk tree takes many years to mature, every Christ follower is, in effect, to exercise faith in God by preparing the way to benefit the faithful who come later.

What have you done so far in life that, like the ancient tamarisk tree Abraham planted, will greatly bless future generations?

How much of a step of faith is it for you to think beyond your needs and put great effort into something that you will not see bear fruit during your lifetime?

What would motivate you to do this day after day?

What impact would it have on your relationship with God?

What might you do today that will provide no benefit to you, but will become a special blessing like the cooling shade of a tall tamarisk tree for those desert travelers who follow after you?

THINK ABOUT IT
Nurturing Fruit for the Future

After the Israelites rebelled in the desert, God disciplined them by forbidding them to enter the Promised Land at that time. He also kept them in the desert until everyone twenty years old or older had died. Certainly that generation of God's people failed often, but they spent up to forty years accomplishing something they would never enjoy the fruit of — training their children and their grandchildren in the ways of the Lord. Their lives focused on those who would follow them, and God blessed their efforts! In effect, their children were their tamarisk trees!

Memorize

> *We will tell the next generation*
> *the praiseworthy deeds of the LORD,*
> *his power, and the wonders he has done.*
> *He decreed statutes for Jacob*
> *and established the law in Israel,*
> *which he commanded our forefathers*
> *to teach their children,*
> *so the next generation would know them,*
> *even the children yet to be born,*
> *and they in turn would tell their children.*
> *Then they would put their trust in God*
> *and would not forget his deeds*
> *but would keep his commands.*

Psalm 78:4 – 7

WHEN YOUR HEART CRIES OUT

At first glance, the desert may seem to have only negative con-
notations in the Bible. Its reputation as a place of danger, death,
suffering, and hardship is well deserved. Even Moses, who spent
most of his life in the desert, described it as that "vast and dreadful
desert, that thirsty and waterless land, with its venomous snakes
and scorpions" (Deuteronomy 8:15).

Pushed by the hardships and uncertainty of the Sinai deserts, the
Israelites soon came to the end of their own strength and resources.
They rebelled against the Lord, murmuring and complaining against
him in spite of his miraculous provision. Because of their rebellion
and lack of trust in God, the desert became a place of punishment
for them.

Yet the desert was also a place of refuge, blessing, and intimate com-
munion with God. When God delivered the Hebrews from slavery
in Egypt, he marched them into the Sinai Desert where he miraculously provided bread from heaven, water from rock, quail, and
protection from their enemies (Exodus 13 – 17). David often found
safety from King Saul's murderous intentions in desert strongholds
(1 Samuel 23:14). Elijah escaped execution by Queen Jezebel by
escaping into the desert (1 Kings 19:1 – 8).

In the barren deserts, God's people experienced many miracles that
turned their times of suffering into intensely personal experiences
of God's glory, guidance, and provision. God chose the desert as his
classroom to teach his people to depend on him as they faced the
painful struggles of each day. There they experienced the Lord's
strength and learned to follow him as their Shepherd, thus becoming equipped with the faith to advance the kingdom of heaven.

Through the desert hardships, God molded his people — Abraham, Moses, the Hebrews, Joshua, David, Jesus, Paul, and many others — into the people they needed to become in order to be his instruments of blessing to all peoples.

The experience of God's care for his people in the wilderness echoes throughout their history: in Moses' last speech (Deuteronomy 2:7), David's songs (Psalm 78), Ezekiel's prophecies (Ezekiel 20), Stephen's speech before the Sanhedrin (Acts 7), and Paul's instruction to the early church (1 Corinthians 10:1 – 13). The Israelites' years of pain and struggle — the years when the hazards of the desert caused them to cry out to God to save them — not only bore fruit in their lives as God molded them, but continue to bear fruit in the lives of God's people who learn from their stories today.

God desires that his people know him intimately, trust him completely, and obey him wholeheartedly so that we can bring his provision and blessing to others who struggle in the deserts of life. But to create such character in us, God sometimes allows or leads us into painful deserts of disease, brokenness, loss, discouragement, rejection, and failure. We may complain and rebel, but when we face the heat, hunger, and thirst of our deserts, when we face the overwhelming floods of adversity, we discover that if we cry out to him for help he will hear our cries and answer.

God is with us! Just as he was present with his ancient people, God is present with us — providing "just enough" to sustain us for another day and another mile. Yes, the desert can be a difficult place that utterly overwhelms us, but it also is the place that drives us back into the arms of our loving, faithful God.

Opening Thoughts (3 minutes)

The Very Words of God

> Save me, O God,
>   for the waters have come up to my neck.
> I sink in the miry depths,
>   where there is no foothold.

> *I have come into the deep waters;*
> *the floods engulf me....*
> *Do not let the floodwaters engulf me*
> *or the depths swallow me up*
> *or the pit close its mouth over me.*
> *Answer me, O Lord, out of the goodness of your love;*
> *in your great mercy turn to me.*
> *Do not hide your face from your servant;*
> *answer me quickly, for I am in trouble.*
>
> *Psalm 69:1 – 2, 15 – 17*

Think About It

Now that you have an idea of what the deserts of the Bible are like, what do you think would be the challenges and dangers of living in or traveling through these deserts? What do you think is the greatest life-threatening danger people face in the desert?

DVD Notes (22 minutes)

Lessons from the desert wadis

Those who build on sand

Those who build on rock

Lessons from floodwaters in the desert

Follow the Shepherd to quiet waters

Cry out to God, who hears and answers

DVD Discussion (7 minutes)

1. Part of this study was filmed in the Judea Wilderness above
   Qumran near the Dead Sea. On the map below, locate the
   Judea Wilderness, Qumran, and the Dead Sea. Rain in the
   mountains, where the cities of Beersheba, Hebron, Bethlehem, and Jerusalem are located, is what causes the flash
   floods in the wadis of the Judea Wilderness. About how far
   away are these mountains from the wilderness wadis near
   the Dead Sea? How would a person in the wilderness know
   that it was raining in the mountains?

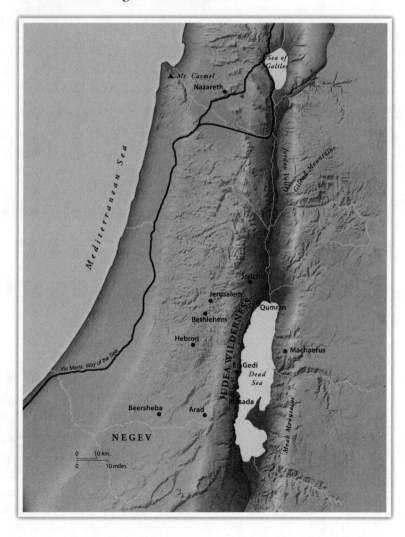

2. In what ways did the video change your understanding of what a flood in a wadi can be like? Of the potential danger of floodwaters in the desert? Of God's watchfulness and power to save when his people call for help?

IT'S HARD TO IMAGINE HOW SUDDEN AND POWERFUL A WADI FLOOD CAN BE.

3. In the desert, some dangers build up gradually and one can see the risk increase to a hazardous level. Other dangers are unexpected, sudden, and dramatic.

   a. What would be some examples of each kind of danger in the desert?

   b. What would be some examples of each kind of danger in the desert experiences of our lives?

4. What did the video add to your understanding of Jesus' parable about building one's house on the sand or on the rock?

   What would be some examples of building on the "sand" today?

   What would be some examples of building on the "rock" today?

5. During biblical times, many of God's people lived near the desert, in the desert, or had traveled through the desert, so the common images from the desert that are used in the Bible helped people to experience God and to be reminded

of him frequently as they went about daily life. To walk on sand is to remember the importance of building on the rock; to step into the sticky mud of a wadi is to remember the Good Shepherd rescuing his sheep and setting them safely on solid ground.

a. In what ways did the desert images shared in the video teach you about God and living in relationship with him?

b. Which images common in your life or the life of your community might God use to teach you, to help you to experience a more vivid relationship with him, or to help you to remember and obey his teaching? For example, what is it about being stuck in traffic and unable to move, experiencing the fury of a hurricane, being amazed by a new technology, or seeing a tornado approach that causes you to say, "That's what it is like when God ____!" or "That is the kind of trouble I was in when God stepped in to save me," or, "When I see ____, it helps me to remember how important it is to obey God and walk with him."

Small Group Bible Discovery and Discussion (21 minutes)

When the Floods of Adversity Sweep over Us

Sometimes life is good in nearly every way, as was true during Solomon's reign when the people "lived in safety, each man under his own vine and fig tree" (1 Kings 4:25). In our world, that picture of the good life may include having a secure job, living in a country that is at peace, having healthy children, and enjoying satisfying relationships. But at other times, life doesn't seem to be very good. In fact, it can become extremely difficult and painful — like life in the desert. We may lose our job, our business may fail, our children may die in battle or by disease, and our relationships may become strained or end. Sometimes we see such desert experiences build slowly to a crisis, but at other times they come at us with startling speed and overwhelming power — like a flood in a desert wadi.

Before becoming king of Israel, David spent much of his life in the Judea Wilderness as a shepherd near Bethlehem and when running for his life from King Saul. So it is not surprising that he included many desert images in his psalms. Let's read the following psalms aloud and see what they reveal to us about David's experience with desert floods and how he trusted God to hear his cry and counted on God to save him.

1. What kind of experience did David compare to a raging flood in Psalm 124:1 - 8?

    What does this psalm add to your understanding of David's life experiences and his trust in God's help?

    Why do you think God allows us to experience "close calls" where we are at risk of being swept away or destroyed before he delivers us?

2. In what ways is David's description of his trouble in Psalm
    69:1 – 3 like a wadi flood, and how serious was the trouble
    he faced?

What do you notice as you continue reading David's plea for
help in verses 13 – 17? To what extent does he seem frantic
or confident about his cry for help and why do you think
that is?

What did David believe was the reason God would help him?
Is it still the reason God helps people? If so, what would you
expect God to do if you cannot avoid a desperate situation
and you cry out to him for help?

THINK ABOUT IT
No Escape from the Floodwaters

To be caught by rushing floodwaters in the bottom of a deep, narrow wadi in
the Judea Wilderness would be a terrifying experience. A few months before
the video for this session was filmed, four hikers died in a flood in the same
canyon in which we stood. The fear we would experience if such a flood
engulfed us became very real. We had no place to run. There was no quick
way to climb up the canyon walls to safety. As we stood in the bottom of that

wadi, we gained a new understanding of Bible passages that mention floods from which there is no escape and recalled experiences in our lives that could be described by a wadi flood.

**A SUDDEN FLOOD IN A WADI SUCH AS THIS
ONE LEAVES FEW OPTIONS FOR ESCAPE.**

3. David composed Psalm 18 after being delivered from enemies who wanted to kill him. Read verses 1 – 6, 16 – 19, 46 – 50.

    a. With which desert images does David describe his desperate situation and God?

b. How does what you have seen of the desert help you to better understand these images, particularly David's life experience with God and the reality of the trouble he faced?

c. What evidence do you see that David had a deep, intimate relationship with God before calamity struck, and how did it help him in the time of crisis?

d. How did David respond to his deliverance, and how does this demonstrate what God wants his people to become through their desert experiences?

4. Which image from the wadis did David use in Psalm 40:1 – 5?

Even though David was apparently at risk as if he were stuck in the muck of a wadi, why do you think he "waited patiently" for the Lord to find him?

How might David's experience as a shepherd have taught him to wait on God, his Shepherd?

What story did David have to share about the trustworthiness of his God?

DID YOU KNOW?
The Mud of the Wadis

Rushing water from the mountains transports heavy, slippery clay into the wadis where it settles in pools in the rock. Baked from the sun, the clay becomes nearly as hard as rock, but when new floods come, the clay softens into a sticky muck that is almost like quicksand. Bedouin shepherds tell stories of sheep that wandered into a wadi to drink and became so stuck in the mud around water pools that their shepherds had to lift them out and set them on rocks above the water. If a flood had come at that time, they all would have drowned. It is likely that David had personal experience rescuing sheep from the mud of wadis in the Judea Wilderness near Bethlehem.

MUDDY AREAS NEAR POOLS OF WATER IN THE BOTTOM OF A WADI POSE A GREAT DANGER TO SHEEP AND OTHER ANIMALS.

Faith Lesson (6 minutes)

Many of us have had to face frightening situations that we cannot escape — situations that fit David's descriptions of being trapped in a raging wadi flood or hopelessly mired in sticky clay. As a teacher, for example, I (Ray) have known parents who have experienced "desert floods" when their child chose paths other than God's path. Whether their child chose sexual experimentation, alcohol, drugs, rebellion, or crime, these parents felt trapped. They could not change their child's path. They could only watch, knowing all too well the disaster that might shatter their lives. Sometimes God spared them such pain, but sometimes the floodwaters of pregnancy, addiction, serious injury, death, or the child's complete rejection of the Christian faith overwhelmed them. When I have shared the images David used to describe his time of crisis, they can relate. Every parent who had experienced this devastation had also "cried out" in fear, helplessness, and even terror.

1. What is your wadi flood? The sudden death of a loved one? An unexpected diagnosis? A devastating breach of trust in a relationship? A crippling financial crisis?

2. How long did you know your difficult time was coming? Did you see the crisis building, or did it crash over you before you knew what was happening?

3. How did it feel to be stuck in the "miry clay" of your circumstances and be unable to avoid or prevent the coming crisis?

In what ways were your feelings like and unlike those David expressed during his times of crisis?

What can you learn from your experience and David's example to help you face a crisis in the future?

4. Did you cry out to God to save you? If not, why not? If so, what did you expect him to do?

How did God rescue you from the crisis or sustain you through the crisis so you were not completely swept away?

5. Why is it important to have a deep and intimate relationship with God *before* tragedy strikes or times of trouble come?

How might you cultivate this kind of relationship with God?

Closing (1 minute)

Read together Psalm 40:1 – 3: "I waited patiently for the LORD; he turned to me and heard my cry. He lifted me out of the slimy pit, out of the mud and mire; he set my feet on a rock and gave me a firm place to stand. He put a new song in my mouth, a hymn of praise to our God. Many will see and fear and put their trust in the LORD."

Then pray about your need for God as you face the dangers of life's deserts. Ask him to strengthen your trust in his love and care for you and to remind you that he is always listening to your call for help when you face difficult circumstances.

Memorize

> *I waited patiently for the LORD;*
> > *he turned to me and heard my cry.*
> *He lifted me out of the slimy pit,*
> > *out of the mud and mire;*
> *he set my feet on a rock*
> > *and gave me a firm place to stand.*
> *He put a new song in my mouth,*
> > *a hymn of praise to our God.*
> *Many will see and fear*
> > *and put their trust in the LORD.*

Psalm 40:1 – 3

Walking with God through Our Deserts

In-Depth Personal Study Sessions

Day One | Sands of the Wadis and the Seashore

The Very Words of God

> *I will surely bless you and make your descendants as numerous as the stars in the sky and as the sand on the seashore. Your descendants will take possession of the cities of their enemies, and through your offspring all nations on earth will be blessed, because you have obeyed me.*
>
> ### *Genesis 22:17 – 18*

Bible Discovery

God Teaches Us through Images of His World

There is little sand in Israel other than in the desert wadis and the beaches of the Mediterranean Sea, yet sand is mentioned as a metaphor or illustration nearly twenty-five times in the Bible. The expression "sand of the seashore" characterizes something that is countless or measureless and communicates clearly to anyone who has seen a sandy beach. The fine-grained sand and clays in the wadis come from erosion of the sandstone and limestone mountains. As rainwater runs down the hillsides and off barren cliffs, it forms torrents of sand and soil-laden water that pass through the wadis. As floodwaters recede and evaporate, the sand settles and fills in depressions in the rock. In ancient times, people gathered this sand to make plaster and glass. So take a look at some of these images and consider how they speak to us from the pages of the Bible.

1. How does the Bible describe the size of the Philistine army that assembled to fight Israel? (See 1 Samuel 13:5 – 7.)

What impact did the size of this army have on the men of Israel, and how does the sand-related metaphor help to create a vivid picture of the situation?

2. Saul was not the first leader of Israel to face a massive assembly of enemies. Consider the situations faced by Joshua (Joshua 11:1 – 5) and Gideon (Judges 7:9 – 12).

    a. What was the meaning of the sand metaphor in these situations, and how might you have felt as an Israelite facing such opposition?

    b. When God's people face opposition that is as impossible to measure as the sand of the seashore, how do you think he wants us to respond?

3. Now read "the rest of the story" of the overwhelming opposition Joshua (Joshua 11:6 – 10) and Gideon (Judges 7:13 – 22) faced.

    a. How did Joshua and Gideon respond, and what relief did God provide in each situation?

b. In what ways do these examples speak to you about God's presence and power in helping his people face seemingly hopeless situations and overwhelming obstacles?

4. Like many rabbis of his day, Jesus used familiar images from daily life to teach about the kingdom of God and what was required to be his disciple. In Matthew 7:21 – 27, he used sand to help illustrate the folly of hearing his words and not putting them into practice.

When Jesus described flooding streams and the wise man building on the rock and the foolish man building on the sand, what kind of location would his listeners have pictured — a place where floods, sand, and rock are found?

Obviously people who lived in Israel recognized the foolishness of building a house on the sand in the bottom of a wadi where violent floods wash away everything in sight! How do you think this image impressed on them the utter foolishness of not practicing what Jesus taught?

With what you have learned about sand and desert wadis, what does this image say to you about your need to faithfully obey Jesus' teachings?

THINK ABOUT IT
Community Is Essential in the Desert

Survival in the desert literally demands that its people care for one another. Even today, Bedouin will say that the unbelievable commitment to hospitality expressed among desert tribes exists in part because as they travel through the barren wilderness they need to depend on others for food, shelter, and especially water. So the code of hospitality is very strong.

In the desert, guests and complete strangers are welcomed and receive the best food and water a family has. Families will serve the last bit of flour they have or defend a guest in their tent with their lives—even if they just met that guest. This code of hospitality is quite foreign to many people in the Western world where privacy, competition, and a spirit of self-sufficiency prevail.

Perhaps it shouldn't surprise us that God chose the desert to be the place where he would prepare his people to be his community of priests who would reveal him to the world. He knew that at times his people would be in the desert, but that far more often they would suffer the intense pain and suffering of life's desert experiences. He would provide manna, shade, and water so that his people would not only survive their desert experiences but as a community—numerous as the sand of the seashore—would share what God had provided them with other people who find themselves in the desert.

5. What "sand" metaphor is used to describe the community of God's people in Genesis 22:15 – 18; Jeremiah 33:22; Hosea 1:10; and Hebrews 11:11 – 12?

How does this image help you to realize the size of the community of God's people?

To what extent have you been encouraged by the size of the community of God's people that has supported you during a time of struggle or pain?

Reflection

Seashore sand beautifully illustrates the nature of God's community of people. Like sand on the seashore, his community is without number. Like sand that sticks together because it is wet by the water of the sea, his community is bound together by his "living water."

God is intent on raising up a great community of people who are to be devoted to the Lord as one, who are to function together in unity, and who are to be supportive of one another. This is the community of blessed hope that leads people to glorify God. This is the great community that God promised to Abraham (Genesis 22:15 – 18). But we must ask ourselves whether we are people who wisely build on the rock or who foolishly build on the sand.

The deep commitment to community found among desert peoples can sometimes be difficult to find among followers of Jesus. It's easy (and sadly, natural) for us to ignore others who struggle and then turn around and seek their help and support during our own desert times. What is necessary for us to become a close-knit, selfless, sympathetic, caring community?

What is your commitment to develop those qualities in yourself, and how are those qualities cultivated in a faith community?

Take time to read and reflect on 1 Corinthians 12:12 – 26, especially verses 12 – 13. What holds the community of God's people together and enables it to function as it should?

If you already are part of a caring faith community, how prepared are you to face desert times and to support others who experience them?

What courage to face tomorrow's unknown struggles does your community provide?

What are some practical ways you and your faith community can live out Jesus' teaching and express the support of God's community to people who are suffering in the midst of desert experiences?

Who do you know who is experiencing a difficult "desert" time and could use the encouragement of God's community?

How willing are you to enter this person's desert and become part of God's provision for him or her?

What specific actions might you take to reach out to this person each month, each week, or maybe each day?

Memorize

May the God who gives endurance and encouragement give you a spirit of unity among yourselves as you follow Christ Jesus, so that with one heart and mouth you may glorify the God and Father of our Lord Jesus Christ. Accept one another, then, just as Christ accepted you, in order to bring praise to God. For I tell you that Christ has become a servant of the Jews on behalf of God's truth, to confirm the promises made to the patriarchs so that the Gentiles may glorify God for his mercy.

Romans 15:5–9

Day Two | When Floodwaters Come

The Very Words of God

> *"Because he loves me," says the* Lord, *"I will rescue him;*
>   *I will protect him, for he acknowledges my name.*
> *He will call upon me, and I will answer him;*
>   *I will be with him in trouble,*
>   *I will deliver him and honor him.*
> *With long life will I satisfy him*
>   *and show him my salvation."*

Psalm 91:14 – 16

Bible Discovery

The Power of Floods to Accomplish God's Purposes

It is hard for us to imagine the terrifying power of floods that occur in the wadis of Israel's deserts, but let's try. On a cloudless day with the blazing sun overhead, the temperature may be well over 100 degrees Fahrenheit as you walk and climb over rocks in the bottom of a dry wadi. You approach a small pool of water just to feel the cooling effect of its moisture, but the clay sucks at your boots and you can hardly take a step.

Then you hear it! A distant rumble that quickly becomes a deep roar. You scramble to climb up the steep rock walls of the wadi and out of danger. Suddenly you see a dust cloud billowing ahead of the first wave of rushing water. Then you see the wave — sometimes inches deep, sometimes feet deep — as it surges through the wadi. Depending on its size, the flood sweeps away anything in its path — rocks and boulders; trees and shrubs; wild animals, sheep, and goats that wandered into the riverbed looking for pools of water from earlier floods; and even travelers or shepherds who were not able to escape. Now you realize how even cars and buses occasionally are washed off roads that cross a wadi.

Floodwaters may flow through a wadi for minutes or for several hours before they diminish. Due to their sudden appearance and awesome, destructive power, it is not surprising that biblical writ-

THE SUDDEN, CATASTROPHIC APPEARANCE OF A WADI FLOOD CAN BE A POWERFUL METAPHOR FOR OUR DESERT EXPERIENCES.

ers used such floods as metaphors and examples of the struggles God's people face in the desert, the drama of God's deliverance and redemption, or the frightening power of his judgment. So come, join the people of the Bible as they learn to know their God and discover his purpose in the floods they experience.

1. The account of Noah and the flood is one of the most familiar stories in the Bible. It is the first account of God using floodwaters to bring judgment against people who refuse to obey or acknowledge him. In what way did the flood also accomplish God's desire to redeem his creation, starting with righteous Noah and his family? (See Genesis 6:11 – 21.)

2. After the Canaanite commander Sisera had oppressed God's people for twenty years, what did they do, and how did God respond? (See Judges 4:1 – 7.)

    How did God destroy Israel's enemy at the Kishon River, which is a wadi that flows only during the floods of the rainy season? (See Judges 4:12 – 16; 5:4, 21.)

    What other time had God rescued his people after they had cried out because of an oppressive ruler, and how was his response as dramatic as a flood in a wadi? (See Exodus 14:21 – 30; 15:1 – 6.)

3. According to 2 Kings 3:1 – 24, the kings of Judah, Israel, and Edom faced a crisis in the desert when they set out to end the rebellion of the king of Moab.

    a. What was the crisis, how serious was it, and where did the kings seek help?

b. What are the indications that God provided a wadi flood
    to deliver his people from their crisis and to execute
    judgment on the army of Moab at the same time?

c. In what sense is the dramatic appearance of floodwaters
    a metaphor for the sudden deliverance that God at times
    provides for suffering people?

4. The writer of Psalm 88 knew what it meant to walk
    through a desert experience. Which metaphors (list
    them!) did he use to describe the difficult circumstances
    God was allowing him to suffer because of his sin? (See
    Psalm 88:1 – 9, 13 – 18.)

    What impact did those circumstances have on him, and
    what was his only source of hope?

    Even though the writer felt that God had abandoned
    him, how often did he call out to God?

What purposes of God do you think might be fulfilled when a person who is feeling overwhelmed by the desert continues to cry out to God for help?

Reflection

Being in a wadi and hearing floodwaters rush toward you is frightening; to have them wash over you is terrifying. As we walk through life, devastating situations sometimes arise like floods and we get trapped in the middle of them. We don't know how to deal with what is happening to us or what it means. We rush to escape, we are frantic for relief, we cling to whatever is near. The floodwaters of pain and suffering are powerful teachers, and as we live through the devastation they bring, we discover who our God is and what we really believe about him.

What are some of the terrible "wadi floods" — perhaps disease, car accident, divorce, death of a child, suicide, economic loss — that have overwhelmed you or someone you love?

How did you respond, and what does your response reveal about your view of God and your relationship with him?

When has God delivered you or someone you love from raging "floodwaters" that otherwise would have swept you away?

How has his response during that time in your life influenced how you view him, how you relate to him, and your hope for the future?

We much prefer to experience comfort, ease, safety, and predictability as opposed to unexpected, sudden, terrifying situations. But what have you learned and how have you experienced God's care and blessing during difficult times that you might not have experienced any other way?

Would you trade that experience for one that was more comfortable? Why or why not?

How do you deal with the pain you experience during "wadi floods" in light of the truth that God uses those same floods to accomplish his good purposes?

Memorize

The Lord is righteous in all his ways
*   and loving toward all he has made.*
The Lord is near to all who call on him,
*   to all who call on him in truth.*
He fulfills the desires of those who fear him;
*   he hears their cry and saves them.*
The Lord watches over all who love him,
*   but all the wicked he will destroy.*

Psalm 145:17 – 20

Day Three | God's People Will Face Floods

The Very Words of God

> Hear my cry, O God;
>> listen to my prayer.
> From the ends of the earth I call to you,
>> I call as my heart grows faint;
>> lead me to the rock that is higher than I.
> For you have been my refuge,
>> a strong tower against the foe.
> I long to dwell in your tent forever
>> and take refuge in the shelter of your wings.
>
> *Psalm 61:1 – 4*

Bible Discovery

They Cried Out to the Lord

We often want God to make our lives comfortable and pain-free. We want to enjoy a life of prosperity, health, and wealth in which we lack nothing. Although God promises a desert-free and flood-free life in the age to come, that is not what he promises for his people on earth — not for his people who lived during biblical times and not for his people today. In this sin-broken world, we will experience desert times; we will be overwhelmed by floods of pain, struggle, suffering, and helplessness. Until the Messiah comes again to restore God's *shalom*, we will face the floods of desert wadis.

When God's ancient people faced difficulties they saw coming or those that crashed over them suddenly with the destructive force of a wadi flood, they cried out to God to deliver them. Often he took them out of their trouble, but at other times he sustained them just enough so that they learned to cling to him, wait on him, and trust him as their Shepherd who would hear their cries and not allow them to be completely swept away.

We also may experience both answers when we cry out to God. Sometimes we are healed, we find a new job, our marriage is restored, our child returns to the Lord, or our loved one overcomes addiction. At other times we live with debilitating pain, cannot find work, face divorce, long for the return of a prodigal child, or watch a loved one self-destruct. No matter what trouble we face, we must learn to cry out to God even when we are weak, exhausted, and see no hope. He may not provide relief exactly as we would like, but he hears our cries and will respond.

1. As you read each of the following passages, identify the "flood" that caused God's people to cry out, then consider how that situation would overwhelm you and how you might respond to it or respond to a similar situation in your life. Then take note of how God responded to their cries for help and consider how his response might deepen your relationship with him.

Text	Why the Person(s) Cried Out	How God Responded
Ex. 14:9–10, 15–18, 24–31		
Ex. 15:22–26		
Num. 11:10–20		
Judg. 3:7–30		
2 Sam. 22:5–7, 17–20		
Ps. 107:1–9		
Jonah 2:1–10		

2. How do we know that God wants us to cry out to him when we need help? (See Luke 18:1 - 8.)

3. God loves all people, but he particularly listens for and responds to the cries of certain people. Whose cries deeply touch the heart of God? (See Exodus 22:22 - 23; Psalms 10:17 - 18; 34:17 - 19; Proverbs 15:29.)

   How does God's care for such people in need encourage you to cry out to him when the floods of life overwhelm you?

4. David faced many overwhelming floods in life, and through those desert experiences he came to know and love God as no other king of Israel. How intimate and honest was he when he cried out to God for help? (See Psalm 55:1 - 8.)

   To what extent do you feel comfortable talking with God as David did — letting everything in your heart spill out to him?

What would help to deepen your relationship with God so that you are able to share all of your concerns and fears with him?

Reflection

Waiting on God — crying out to him but not immediately receiving the answer we expect — is hard for us. We tend to want to fix things. If we can't solve the problems we face in life ourselves, surely we can find an expert to make things right! But God's priority is not to remove our difficulties; it is to mold and shape us to be his partners who trust him completely and have a heart that is like his own.

To develop such intimacy with God, we sometimes need to patiently wait and continue to cry out even when we are exhausted. The discipline of calling out to God when we face overwhelming floods creates within us a passion to know him, to understand his ways, and to trust him no matter how difficult our path. Psalm 77 provides a beautiful picture of this process. Take time to read and meditate on this psalm and see what you discover about your God.

How great was the psalmist's distress, and when have you felt similar distress?

How close do you think the psalmist was to giving up hope that God would save him, and when have you felt similar desperation?

What revived the psalmist's hope?

What did the psalmist "relearn" about how God hears and answers the cries of his people when God didn't instantly solve his problem?

Do you think this was God's answer to his cry for help? Why or why not?

In what ways does remembering what God has done for his people when they have cried out to him in the past help you to trust and wait on God to respond to your cries for help today?

Memorize

I cried out to God for help;
 I cried out to God to hear me.
When I was in distress, I sought the Lord;
 at night I stretched out untiring hands
 and my soul refused to be comforted....
"Will the Lord reject forever?
 Will he never show his favor again?

Has his unfailing love vanished forever?
    Has his promise failed for all time?
Has God forgotten to be merciful?
    Has he in anger withheld his compassion?"
Then I thought, "To this I will appeal:
    the years of the right hand of the Most High."
I will remember the deeds of the Lord*;*
    yes, I will remember your miracles of long ago.
I will meditate on all your works
    and consider all your mighty deeds.

Psalm 77:1 – 2, 7 – 12

Day Four | Wadi Floods: A Metaphor for Life

The Very Words of God

Say to those with fearful hearts,
    "Be strong, do not fear;
your God will come,
    he will come with vengeance;
with divine retribution
    he will come to save you."
Then will the eyes of the blind be opened
    and the ears of the deaf unstopped.
Then will the lame leap like a deer,
    and the mute tongue shout for joy.
Water will gush forth in the wilderness
    and streams in the desert.
The burning sand will become a pool,
    the thirsty ground bubbling springs.

Isaiah 35:4 – 7

Bible Discovery

Desert Images Lead Us to Reflect on Our Life with God

Biblical writers drew from myriad images of their physical world — plants and animals, deserts and fertile hillsides, planets and stars, wind and rain, mountains and valleys — to describe their theological beliefs about life, God, and what it meant to live in relationship with him. For example, they likened God's endurance to that of the sun (Psalm 72:5), his righteousness to mighty mountains (Psalm 36:6), his provision for his people to that of a shepherd (Psalm 23:1), and his revelation to humanity to the rain and snow that water the earth (Isaiah 55:10 – 11). To this day, people of the Middle East use metaphors from the physical world to present theological truth.[1]

It is not surprising that biblical writers used desert wadis and the seasonal floods that roared through them as metaphors for times of adversity and sudden disaster in life. What may surprise us is that the biblical writers also used images of desert wadis and surging floodwaters to describe God's overwhelming love and blessing. So take a look at some of the ways images of desert wadis can lead us to think about life and how God wants us to live it in relationship with him.

1. When God created the universe, he established *shalom* —
    peace, unity, and harmony — on the earth. As Creator, he has
    power over his creation. As the maker of humankind, he has
    a heart that desires to bless his people and bring *shalom* into
    their lives.

    a. Which powerful image of the desert wadis did the
        psalmist use to describe the judgment God brought on
        his people because of their sin? (See Psalm 107:33 – 34.)

    b. What did God then do in the desert and wadis to express
        his love and to bless those who had suffered in life? (See
        Psalm 107:35 – 38, 43.)

c. In what ways have some of your life experiences been like these contrasting images, when God has removed his blessing and allowed you to struggle and suffer pain and then restored you like water restores life to the desert?

2. What state of injustice and oppression concerned God in Amos 5:4 – 15?

How greatly did this situation offend God, and what did it lead him to do? (See Amos 5:21 – 23.)

Which metaphor of desert wadis was used to describe what God desired to see happen? (See Amos 5:24.)

How do you imagine the sudden appearance of a powerful, roaring river of justice would change this situation? How would it change injustices in your culture?

3. After a period of desert experiences when many of God's
    people did not follow him, which images of a flooding wadi
    did Isaiah use to describe the rich blessings God promised
    to restore to Jerusalem (where God's presence lived in the
    temple, where they experienced him in community) and its
    people? (See Isaiah 66:12 – 14.)

    How do these images help you to comprehend the abun-
    dance of God's blessing that he desires his people to enjoy?

4. In Psalm 42:1 – 2, what image did the psalmist use to
    describe a godly person's thirst for God and his blessings?

    In what environment would great thirst be an ongoing issue?

    Where in the desert are such streams found?

    How well does this metaphor capture what your relationship
    with God means to you in the midst of your life's deserts?

IT'S A BLESSING TO FIND A STREAM IN A DESERT WADI.

Reflection

There is a sense in which life is like a desert wadi in which we experience both overwhelming adversity and overflowing blessing. Sometimes our desert experiences nearly consume us, and we feel numb to any blessing. At other times, blessings trickle in and save us like water from a life-giving desert spring. And on some occasions, blessings rush over us like floodwaters in a wadi, washing away our grief, pain, weariness, and doubts.

Job was a godly man who, through no fault of his own, endured a series of terrible desert experiences. His distress and confusion led him to reflect deeply on every aspect of life and every nuance of his relationship with God. At one point he reflected on the brevity of life using metaphors of desert wadis: "Man born of woman is of few days and full of trouble. He springs up like a flower and withers away; like a fleeting shadow, he does not endure.... he breathes his last and is no more. As water disappears from the sea or a riverbed becomes parched and dry, so man lies down and does not rise" (Job 14:1 – 2, 10 – 12).

I (Ray) have had times of reflection similar to Job's since my mother's death in an auto accident and my heart attack. Sudden tragedy can bring on a deep awareness of how swiftly life passes or how fragile it is. Although God's strength was more than sufficient during those times, the sense of life's fragility — what Job described as a riverbed that becomes parched and dry — often overwhelmed me. During more joyful times of blessing, such reflections have occurred when my children or grandchildren stepped into a new stage of life: starting school, having their first date, graduating from school, going to college, marrying, and having children. These events also trigger an awareness of life's sweet but sudden passing.

When have you had moments like Job when you realized how tenuous life is?

What happened to lead you to reflect on the reality of your life and God's place in it?

Did your reflections bring you closer to him? Why or why not?

When have you experienced just a life-saving trickle of blessing from God that touched you deeply and inspired you to reflect on your relationship with him?

When have you experienced the rushing floods of God's blessing and restoration after a time of struggle?

How did you respond to God, and what did you realize about
your relationship with him?

Day Five | The Wadis: A Picture of God's Shalom

The Very Words of God

> *The poor and needy search for water,*
>   *but there is none;*
>   *their tongues are parched with thirst.*
> *But I the L<small>ORD</small> will answer them;*
>   *I, the God of Israel, will not forsake them.*
> *I will make rivers flow on barren heights,*
>   *and springs within the valleys.*
> *I will turn the desert into pools of water,*
>   *and the parched ground into springs.*
>
>   *Isaiah 41:17 – 18*

Bible Discovery

God Is Restoring His Creation

Many biblical writers wrote prophetically about the coming age of
God's *shalom* — the restoration of harmony and peace God desires
for his people. Sometimes these writers used the wadi metaphor of
flooding streams to portray God's coming redemption. Some of their
prophecies have been partly fulfilled; others await God's continuing work through history. As you conclude this session, look for the

hope of restoration that only God can provide. Although you may be inclined to focus on when and how these promises will be fulfilled, try to focus on the writers' description of the *shalom* God promises.

1. How did Isaiah describe God's coming *shalom*? Make a list of the desert images you recognize. (See Isaiah 35:1 – 7.)

   What taste of the *shalom* that God will one day bring to all things has he brought into the deserts of your life?

   In what ways has this taste of *shalom* been for you like a blossoming crocus, a rushing stream, or a bubbling spring in the desert?

2. What did the Lord God do for his people after their time of great suffering in the desert of exile? (See Psalm 126:1 – 6.)

   What impact did this restoration of fortune have on God's people and on the witnessing nations?

When the psalmist compared their restoration to streams in the Negev (remember, the Negev is the desert region south of the mountains of Judea), what was he saying about the intensity and drama of what God had done?

3. It is wonderful when God graciously pours out his physical and material blessing on his people, but *shalom* also involves the restoration of God's people to their rightful relationship with him. How dramatic, powerful, and life-changing did Isaiah say the outpouring of God's blessing and Spirit will be? (See Isaiah 44:1 – 5.)

    How does this image help you to understand God's *shalom* and the hope he promises?

4. According to Isaiah 32:1 – 2, what did God promise for the future?

    Jewish readers would understand a reign of righteousness and justice to mean the coming of the kingdom of God (heaven), the restoration of *shalom*. What will each person become at that time?

Reflection

Job was a righteous man who trusted God, and because of that experienced a flood of terribly painful disasters. During those trials, Job did not renounce his faith in the Lord as Satan had desired, but he certainly longed for relief, understanding, comfort, and encouragement. For a long time, God seemed to offer Job nothing — no deliverance, no explanation — so his God-fearing friends came to comfort him.

> What kind of "comfort" did Job actually receive from his three friends, and which metaphor did he use to describe his disappointment in them? (See Job 6:14 – 17.)

> What do you think Job hoped his friends would be to him, and what might you have hoped for if you were in Job's situation?

> What do you think God would have desired for Job, and why?

When the kingdom of God (heaven) comes in all its fullness, each person will be like a shelter from the wind, a refuge from the storm, and a stream of water in the desert (Isaiah 32:2). Until that day, God desires that his people — following the example of Jesus — be like streams of living water in the desert and bring a refreshing taste of God's *shalom* to those who are weary and thirsty.

> Would people who know you well describe you as being like a stream of water in the desert? Why or why not?

God's great desire is to restore *shalom* to his creation. Sometimes we see glimpses of this. At other times such a powerful redemptive work seems far away, overshadowed by life's deserts. Even though we may not see it, God continues his redemptive work. One day those who follow Christ will experience the overflowing joy and blessing of God's kingdom. Until then, God will continue to pour out his blessings and call his people to be like streams of water in the desert.

> Which metaphors of the *shalom* God promises in the future encourage you and bring you hope during your difficult desert times?

> In what ways can you share this hope with others who are experiencing desert times?

Memorize

> *I, the God of Israel ... will make rivers flow on barren heights,*
> *and springs within the valleys.*
> *I will turn the desert into pools of water,*
> *and the parched ground into springs.*

> *Isaiah 41:17 – 18*

THEY WERE NOT WANDERING

What an amazing year the Hebrews experienced while camped at the foot of Mount Sinai. It was one of the most momentous years in the history of God's people. Every morning, manna covered the ground. In a waterless land, water gushed out of solid rock. Then the Lord, Creator of the universe, descended onto the mountain in thunder and lightning, smoke and earthquake. From there he spoke the "Ten Words" (Ten Commandments) — the vows that united the Creator and his chosen people like a husband and his bride. In unity, obedience, gratitude, and love, God's people gave the best of what they had to build the tabernacle as the place for God's presence to reside among them.

Then it was time to move on. The pillar of cloud lifted from the tabernacle and moved ahead of the people, leading them on the unknown (to them) path to the Promised Land. Because of their stubborn resistance and outright rebellion, however, the journey through the Wilderness of Paran stretched to forty years. Most of God's people who began the journey died on the way. But those who were young when they left Mount Sinai and the children who were born in the wilderness emerged from their journey as a community of God's people who were ready to take the next step in his redemptive plan.

We often refer to this period in Israel's history as "wandering" through the wilderness. In one sense, this is true: "The Lord's anger burned against Israel and he made them wander in the desert" (Numbers 32:13). But the Israelites were never lost during this time; their movements were not without purpose or direction. The Bible emphasizes that during this time God led his people as a shepherd leads a flock. The people moved when and where God desired. Moses summarized the Israelites' experience by saying, "Remember how the LORD your God led you all the way in the desert these forty years" (Deuteronomy 8:2).

Life for God's people is always like this. We know our eternal destination, but as we walk through our daily lives we rarely know exactly where we are going, how to get there, or when we will arrive. We must seek the right path and follow it faithfully, trusting God to lead us to the destination he has promised as he molds us into the people he desires us to be.

When Jesus called his disciples, saying, "Come, follow me" (Matthew 4:19), they trusted that he would lead them to the place he had prepared for them. But their journey was a walk of faith that led into the unknown. How often were they confused or uncertain about the path they walked as they fulfilled their mission of being God's witnesses to the world? We know that Paul desired to go to Rome and that God prevented it until the apostle went in chains! Perhaps he wondered about the path too, but he trusted that God was leading him and continued walking.

It must be the same for us. In a world shaped by fear, uncertainty, and insecurity, we must seek God's path and follow him obediently into the unknown. Although we may travel through difficult and painful deserts, God guides our every step without necessarily revealing the next. We sometimes may feel that we wander aimlessly, but God is watching and guiding our way. Like God's people who have gone before us, we are not wandering, we are led!

Opening Thoughts (3 minutes)

The Very Words of God

> By day you led them with a pillar of cloud, and by night with a pillar of fire to give them light on the way they were to take.
>
> **Nehemiah 9:12**

Think About It

When we talk about life, we often speak of it as a path. We may say, "I decided to _____, but I didn't know where that path would lead," or, "When _____ happened, I realized I was on the wrong path."

When have you thought that you lost your way on the path of life, and how did you know something was wrong?

What are the signs you look for to know that you are following the right path?

DVD Notes (26 minutes)

God led his people on a path no one had walked before

Life is to be a walk on God's path

Jesus is the ancient path to God

We walk the path in community *with* God

God's path may be rough and rocky, but he is there

DVD Discussion (7 minutes)

1. The Israelites walked on many different paths as they made
    their way to the Promised Land. The different paths you
    have seen in this video series are much like the paths they
    walked. (The path filmed for this study is in the southern
    Sinai Peninsula near Jebel Katarina and Jebel Musa, the tradi-
    tional Mount Sinai.)

    Look at the map on page 193 and consider the topography of
    the different regions through which they passed. Some paths
    may have followed the shores of the Red Sea (Gulf of Suez
    and Gulf of Aqaba). Some may have twisted through sandy
    wadis, others over rocky mountain passes. On some paths
    their destination may have been in view; on others they may
    have thought they were wandering into the unknown.

    What did you imagine these paths looked like before you
    saw the video?

To what extent did the difficulty of the paths through the desert surprise you?

What do you think it might have been like to follow God and learn from him as you walked on these paths?

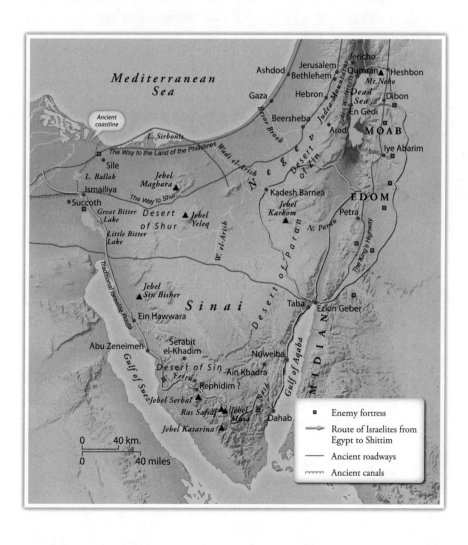

2. Although we may say Israel *wandered* through the desert, the truth is God *led* them every step of the way. In what ways does wandering on the path of life differ from being led by God? Does it look different? Feel different? Lead to a different place?

3. When you consider the varied paths that people walk through life, does it seem to you that most people walk as wanderers or as people who arc being led? Why?

   To what extent do you think people today would notice the way Jesus walked his path (lived his life) as John the Baptist noticed it, and what would they recognize as being different?

   What do you think people today notice about the way you walk the path of life? Would they recognize that you walk with God? Why or why not?

4. How would you describe the path on which God desires his people to walk? What is it like? What must one do to discover it? What is required to stay on it? Where does it lead?

5. When you have encountered painful obstacles on a rough, steep, dangerous path, have you found the honey in the rock and tasted the goodness of God? If so, how did that sweet moment encourage you, and how can it encourage others?

Small Group Bible Discovery and Discussion (18 minutes)

Walk the Right Path

Many times the Bible mentions ordinary paths — the routes a person walked in order to travel from one place to another — as a metaphor to describe human experience and God's intentions for his people. To walk on a path, both literally and figuratively, involves choosing it and remaining on it until the individual arrives at the intended destination. So the paths on which we choose to "walk" (or "live," in our English usage) reveal our focus and portray the character of our lives. We either walk on God's path and choose to obey and trust him faithfully, or we take another path and make different choices. Let's explore the two main paths emphasized in the Bible — God's path (the way of the righteous) and the path (way) of the sinner.

1. The Bible is full of instruction for walking life's path. It tells us how to find God's path and describes the benefits of walking on it. It also warns us against the dangers of walking the path of wickedness or evil. The following passages provide a very brief overview of the Bible's teaching. Read each one and see what you learn about following God's path and walking in his ways as opposed to following the path of sin. Using the chart on page 196, write down your observations about the paths one may choose in life so that you build a picture or profile of each. (See Psalms 1:6; 16:11; 18:30 – 36; Proverbs 2:6 – 22; 4:10 – 22, 26 – 27; 14:12; 15:9; 28:18.)

	God's Path	The Other Path
Who walks on each path?		
What is each path like and what happens on it?		
What are the benefits or dangers of each path?		
How does God view those who walk on each path?		
What does God do for those who walk on each path?		
What is the destiny of each path and the people who choose to walk on it?		

What did you learn about God's path or the path of wickedness that you did not realize before?

How different are the two paths, and how much do you think it matters which path you choose?

2. When the Israelites were at last ready to enter the Promised Land, they were well trained in walking God's path. Yet Moses was still concerned about the path they might choose in the future. In his final plea for them to keep walking on God's path, how did he describe the difference between the two paths? (See Deuteronomy 30:15 – 19.)

   Are his pleas and warnings effective enough to convince you? Why or why not?

3. What was the psalmist's attitude toward each path? (See Psalm 119:30 – 35, 101 – 105, 127 – 128.)

   What delight and joy did walking God's path bring into the psalmist's life?

   How eagerly did he seek to know God's path and follow it wherever it might lead?

What would you say if you were asked to describe what walking God's path means to you?

THINK ABOUT IT
A Path Is Not a Road!

In the modern world, we can travel from place to place on roads that are mapped, designed, and constructed using the latest technology and equipment. We can know where a road will lead and how fast we can travel on it before it is even built. The biblical understanding of a path is not a constructed road, however. The Hebrew word translated "path" is derived from the word translated "cart" and refers to the ruts left when carts pass over an area multiple times. So a path is a furrow(s) that is cut into the ground during a long period of time as animals and people pass over it.

God's path is not the product of abstract, two-dimensional maps. His path is the route he intends his people to walk as they live in obedience to his every word. It is the path that God himself walked when Jesus became one of us. To walk God's path is, in a sense, like placing our feet in the ruts worn by the faithful, godly people who have gone before us.[1]

Faith Lesson (5 minutes)

For forty years, the ancient Hebrews — as we often say and they may have thought — "wandered" through the desert. Although they may not have known where they were going or how to get there, they never truly wandered because God led them. Whenever the pillar of cloud and fire moved, God's people followed. We do not have the visual symbol of a pillar to follow, but through his Word God continues to instruct people in how to walk his path (Isaiah 2:1 – 3). His Word is our "pillar," leading us every step of the way.

1. How would you describe the two main "paths" of life — the way of the righteous (God's path) and the way of sinners, and on which path do you want to walk?

    Do you sometimes walk on one of these paths, then switch to the other? If so, how might you correct your course and stay on the path you truly desire? If not, what keeps you walking in the path you desire?

2. For people who desire to walk God's path today, the crucial questions are: "How well do you know God's Word?" and "How committed are you to learning God's ways from his Word?"

    a. Do you know it well enough to be led by it when you are uncertain as to what will happen around the next bend?

    b. Do you know it well enough to be led by it when you feel that you are wandering or have lost your way?

    c. Do you know it well enough to trust its leading even when your feelings or the counsel of others seem to suggest another path?

    d. What do these responses indicate you might need to change about your relationship to God's Word?

3. In Psalm 119:97 – 105, the psalmist expresses his love for God's law (which is another way of saying God's Word) and how obedience to it keeps him on the right path.

    a. If you have ever sensed that God is leading you, what encouragement did you receive to continue on despite the difficulties and obstacles on the path, and to what extent did his leading cause you to more eagerly study and know his Word?

    b. When in your life has God's Word been a light that guided you on his path? What might have happened if you had not had that light, and to what extent has that experience led you to eagerly seek God's light for every step you take?

Closing (1 minute)

Read together Psalm 119:101 – 105: "I have kept my feet from every evil path so that I might obey your word. I have not departed from your laws, for you yourself have taught me. How sweet are your words to my taste, sweeter than honey to my mouth! I gain understanding from your precepts; therefore I hate every wrong path. Your word is a lamp to my feet and a light for my path."

Then pray, asking God to help you choose his path daily. Commit to him your passionate desire to know and obey his Word. Ask him to guide your feet moment by moment and day by day so that you do not depart from the right path.

Memorize

> *I have kept my feet from every evil path*
> *so that I might obey your word.*
> *I have not departed from your laws,*
> *for you yourself have taught me.*
> *How sweet are your words to my taste,*
> *sweeter than honey to my mouth!*
> *I gain understanding from your precepts;*
> *therefore I hate every wrong path.*
> *Your word is a lamp to my feet*
> *and a light for my path.*
>
> ***Psalm 119:101 – 105***

Walking with God through Our Deserts

In-Depth Personal Study Sessions

Day One | The Paths We Walk

The Very Words of God

> *I will lead the blind by ways they have not known,*
> *along unfamiliar paths I will guide them;*
> *I will turn the darkness into light before them*
> *and make the rough places smooth.*
> *These are the things I will do;*
> *I will not forsake them.*
>
> Isaiah 42:16

Bible Discovery

Ups and Downs on Life's Path

To walk God's path is the most amazing adventure a person can experience in life. When we walk God's path, we choose to live in obedience to his words and commands and thereby experience a life-giving relationship with the Creator of the universe! As we walk his path, we come under his watchful care, protection, and provision. This is not to say that our path — meaning the experiences we have in life — will always be easy and enjoyable. If we choose the righteous, life-giving path as opposed to the path of sin and wickedness, we still have to deal with the variety of life experiences that occur on our path through life.

1. Think about the forty years the Israelites spent walking from Egypt to the Promised Land. There is no doubt that God was leading them, but their path wasn't always smooth and pleasant. Yes, sometimes the path became difficult when they rebelled and stepped off God's path to pursue their own

desires, but even when they were faithfully walking the path God put before them it wasn't easy. Some sections of the path were difficult and dangerous.

a. According to the following texts, what were some of the more painful parts of the path on which the Israelites walked, and how did God provide for his people during these times?

Exodus 14:10 – 12, 19 – 28

Exodus 15:22 – 25

Exodus 16:1 – 3, 11 – 16

Exodus 17:8 – 16

Numbers 21:4 – 9

b. According to the following texts, what pleasant stretches of God's path did the Israelites experience, and how did these times encourage them when the path became more difficult?

Exodus 15:27

Exodus 18:5 – 14

Exodus 19:1 – 8, 16 – 17

Exodus 24:1 – 12

Exodus 25:8 – 9; 40:1 – 2, 33 – 38

c. In what ways do some of the extreme experiences Israel
    encountered provide insight into your life's experiences?

THINK ABOUT IT

What Does It Mean to Walk a Desert Path?

God led the Israelites through the deserts of Sinai, the Wilderness of Paran,
the Negev, and the Wilderness of Zin. The typical terrain in these desert
regions is steep, rocky mountains separated by scattered valleys. In some
areas the mountains are higher than others, and in other areas the valleys
are deeper and more narrow than others. Typically there is little or no topsoil
and very little rainfall, so there are few plants.

Ancient trails still crisscross these deserts, but walking across them remains
a challenge. Most people travel in the valleys and bottoms of the wadis

because the mountains are too steep and high to cross easily. Much of the open landscape is strewn with rocks, so to travel any distance at all requires difficult climbing. Each step involves choosing where to put your foot, the effort to take the step, and deciding where your next step will be. It is certainly not like strolling through a tree-shaded park on a flat sidewalk!

During biblical times, few people could afford to ride animals such as donkeys or horses, so they walked. They walked frequently from their villages to their terraced gardens, to pasture land, or to work their trades. Often they walked longer distances — twenty, fifty miles or more — for the annual festivals in Jerusalem, to conduct business, to visit relatives, or to seek healing from their diseases.

So it was natural that the metaphor of "walking a path" came to symbolize one's passage through life. Rather than saying *life* or *living*, someone from biblical times might say *walk* or *walking*. Whereas we would say "live a good life," they would say "walk a good walk." They understood that life, like walking, was sometimes easy and sometimes very hard.

When people visit Israel today, a short walk on a well-maintained sidewalk often leads from the tour bus to the exact location — Caesarea, Capernaum, Beth Shan — where biblical events took place. Although these stops are worth

continued on next page . . .

WALKING THE DESERT PATH IS NOT AN EASY STROLL.

every minute, visitors who are willing to get off the modern roads can still find the ancient trails that lead to sites such as upper En Gedi, Gamla, or the Wilderness of Zin. The arduous hikes on narrow paths that are required to reach these locations give a more realistic portrayal of what it means to walk God's path.

2. God has promised to watch, protect, and provide for his people as they walk his path. Because we know God is faithful to his promises, we tend to think that he always will make our way easy and smooth. But just as the paths on which we walk from place to place lead up steep hills, over rough ground, and through pleasant places, our life's path takes us through times of danger, pain, and pleasure. As you read the following accounts, consider some of the good and bad times God's people have encountered on life's path. Take note of how God faithfully protected and provided in all situations.

   a. What risks did the Israelites face just by being in the desert, and how did God meet their needs? (See Nehemiah 9:19 – 21.)

b. Job was thrust onto such a difficult path that he felt
    abandoned by God. What good things did he remember
    experiencing because God had watched over him in the
    past? (See Job 29:2 - 6.)

c. What difficult challenges did David face on his path, and
    what did God do to help him succeed in light of them?
    (See 2 Samuel 22:17 - 20, 33 - 37.)

d. What kinds of paths did David say God led him through?
    Were they all easy? What made it possible for David to
    walk where they led? (See Psalm 23:1 - 4.)

e. On what kinds of paths are we inclined to stumble, and
    where is God when we face those dangerous paths? (See
    Psalm 37:23 - 24.)

f. What are the dangers of unfamiliar paths, darkness, and
    rough places, and what will God do for those who faith-
    fully seek to walk his path? (See Isaiah 42:16.)

Reflection

When you consider all that God has promised to do for his faithful people as they walk life's path, and see the ways (as in the preceding examples) by which he has actually fulfilled those promises, our path must be a bit rough in places! In fact, the wisdom of Proverbs describes God as "a shield to those whose walk is blameless, for he guards the course of the just and protects the way of his faithful ones" (Proverbs 2:7 – 8). It sounds like God fights very hard on behalf of his people to help them walk on difficult paths.

Review each of the examples in question two and think about ways in which God has provided for you when you have walked through difficult stretches on life's path. How, for example, did he:

Sustain you for a long period of time when you lacked some of the basic necessities of life — food, water, clothing, health, etc.?

Hold you up when your own steps faltered?

Lead you and prepare the way when you could not see what was ahead?

Bring times of relief and blessing that made you long for him when times seemed too difficult to bear?

As you think about the painful stretches on your life's path, how does God's care and presence help you to continue to walk his path no matter what lies ahead?

Memorize

O people of Zion, who live in Jerusalem, you will weep no more. How gracious he will be when you cry for help! As soon as he hears, he will answer you.... Whether you turn to the right or to the left, your ears will hear a voice behind you, saying, "This is the way; walk in it."

Isaiah 30:19, 21

Day Two | Know the Path and Choose It

The Very Words of God

This is what the Lord says:
"Stand at the crossroads and look;
*   ask for the ancient paths,*
ask where the good way is, and walk in it,
*   and you will find rest for your souls."*

Jeremiah 6:16

Bible Discovery

God's Path Calls Us to Take Action: Walk in It!

We each have a certain lifestyle or life to live, which someone from Jesus' day would be likely to describe as a "path" on which we "walk." God has a path or way that he walks too, and he wants us to walk it with him. In the very first story in the Bible, God walked on the earth in harmonious fellowship with the people he created (Genesis 3:8 - 9). He still desires for people to live, or, as the biblical language prefers, *walk*, in harmony with him. Unfortunately, many people who look for God's path have no intention of walking it.

They may know a great deal about it, perhaps even tell others how to walk it, but they stop short of walking it themselves. Therefore, they do not find the harmony ("rest for your souls," Jeremiah 6:16) that comes from walking in God's path.

1. When giving the law to the Israelites, Moses clearly explained how to walk in harmony with God. (See Leviticus 26:3 – 12.)

   a. What is the fundamental choice a person must make in order to walk with God? (v. 3)

   b. God will bless his people in amazing ways if they choose to walk in his path, but what is the greatest blessing of all? (v. 12)

   c. In what ways is the portrayal of the blessings God promised to pour out if his people walked with him an image of the *shalom* — harmony, unity, peace — God desires all people to experience?

2. What kind of life or path did the prophet Jeremiah call God's people to search for, and why? (See Jeremiah 6:16.)

Why is knowing *about* the ancient path not sufficient for finding rest, and what is crucial to living in harmony with God where one's soul finds rest?

What are the consequences of refusing to walk in the ancient path, and which other path could those consequences describe? (See Jeremiah 6:18 – 21.)

3. When Jesus invited people to come to him and take on his "yoke," which meant to obey his teachings, what did he say they would find? (See Matthew 11:28 – 30.)

In light of Jeremiah 6:16, what was Jesus saying about himself in relationship to the ancient path?

If we want to walk in God's path — the ancient path that gives rest to our souls — how important is it that we obey Jesus' teachings?

DID YOU REALIZE?

When Jesus Walked

The oldest Greek manuscripts of John 1:36 literally read, "When he [John the Baptist] saw Jesus *walking*, he said, 'Look the lamb of God.' " This suggests that John observed far more than Jesus walking into view. Although it cannot be proven, it seems that when John saw the obedient, righteous walk of Jesus, he immediately recognized that anyone who walked like that must be the Messiah who walked with God!

Certainly by his sacrifice on the cross and miraculous resurrection, Jesus provided the way (Hebrew, *derekh*) or path to God. He became "the way and the truth and the life" (John 14:6). But that's not all. In the person of Jesus the Messiah, God walked with us! In person, he showed us what his path looks like and how to walk in it. He came to be God with us, walking side by side with people as he did with Adam and Eve.

4.   When Jesus called his first disciples, how quickly did they obey his words and follow (walk) in his path? (See Matthew 4:18 – 22.)

What did the disciples consider to be the difference between *knowing* Jesus' commands and *obeying* them, and why did they want to obey his commands and walk as he walked? (See 1 John 2:3 – 6.)

Do you think Jesus' disciples viewed following in his path in the same way they viewed walking in God's path as they understood it from the Hebrew Bible? Why or why not?

5. Obedience is central to walking God's path, and God's people must make significant life choices in order to walk that path. What are some of those choices, and what good things, harmony, and rest does God promise we will experience when we walk in his path? Make a list based on the following portions of the Bible — Deuteronomy 5:28 – 33; 26:16 – 18; 28:9; Psalms 84:11 – 12; 119:30 – 32; Micah 6:8; Colossians 3:1 – 7.

    Then add to your list some personal choices you need to make in order to walk faithfully in God's path. For example, you may need to abandon some of the ways, as Colossians says, you used to walk "in the life you once lived." And remember, we're not just to *know* the path, God wants us to *walk it with him.*

The life choices we must make to walk with God on his path:	The harmony, good things, and "rest for your souls" that God promises to those who walk his path:

6. During the coming age of Messiah, when God's *shalom* will
    be restored, what will people from all nations go to Jerusa-
    lem to find? (See Isaiah 2:2 – 3.)

What will God teach them, and for what purpose?

In what way does walking in God's path always portray his
shalom — in the garden of Eden, in the desert wilderness, in
your world, and in the future?

Reflection

The Bible emphasizes the importance of obeying God and walking
his path in steadfast commitment rather than simply knowing about
his path. Faith is not just a set of beliefs and doctrines. It is practiced
belief shaped by the words and commands of God. To be a faithful
follower of God is to put his way of living into practice by applying
his commandments to one's daily walk.

Too often, however, we are content to study God's path. We define
it, proof-text it, enshrine it in creeds and statements of faith, teach it
to children, memorize it, and even separate from other people over
it. But this is not how we live it! God is not satisfied when we simply
know the truth intellectually. In the biblical context, to know God
is to experience him. Thus God desires that we *halak* his *derekh* —
walk, live, obey his path. Or, in the language of the early Christians,
if we claim to be in him, we must walk as Jesus walked (1 John 2:6).

What does it mean to you that God desires to "walk" with you as
you walk in his path?

If you have never pictured walking with God to be a personal, side-by-side experience like that of Adam and Eve with God in the garden of Eden or like the disciples experiencing life as Jesus walked it every day, how has this study helped you to realize the kind of life relationship God desires to have with you?

How do you think a daily, more intimate walk with God on his path would help you to experience a bit more peace, hope, and rest as you encounter the difficult as well as the pleasant times in life?

Why would you say it is insufficient for God's people merely to know *about* his path?

What do we need to know about God's path in order to walk it?

What do we "gain" by obediently walking the path *with* him?

How do we keep learning his path and how to walk in it?

What is your greatest weakness or obstacle to walking in God's
path, and what are you willing to cast aside or to pursue in order
to walk with him in all his ways?

Memorize

And now, O Israel, what does the Lord *your God ask of you but to fear
the* Lord *your God, to walk in all his ways, to love him, to serve the* Lord
your God with all your heart and with all your soul, and to observe the
Lord's *commands and decrees that I am giving you today for your own
good?*

Deuteronomy 10:12 – 13

Day Three | Walking God's Path Prepares the Way

The Very Words of God

In the desert prepare the way for the Lord;
>   *make straight in the wilderness a highway for our God.*
Every valley shall be raised up,
>   *every mountain and hill made low;*
the rough ground shall become level,
>   *the rugged places a plain.*
And the glory of the Lord *will be revealed,*
>   *and all mankind together will see it.*
For the mouth of the Lord *has spoken.*

Isaiah 40:3 – 5

Bible Discovery

The Righteous Prepare the Way of the Lord

God has prepared a path, or way, for us to walk, and we walk that
path by obeying his Word, the Bible. When we walk in God's path,

he promises to bless us and to walk with us. But for God to come and walk with us, we must prepare the way, and we do that by walking in his path — a lot.

God's way is not prepared when we walk his path occasionally. The Hebrew word that Isaiah used for God's "path" (*derekh*) can mean a major road — a highway — or a path that is worn by *constant* walking. So the way of the Lord is prepared by an ongoing, obedient walk on God's path. It is prepared by repentance and rededication to righteous living. Isaiah promised that when the way was prepared by such a walk, the glory of the Lord — his awesome presence — would appear.

During biblical times, righteous people valued their walk with God so highly that some of them went into the desert to seek God's forgiveness and to devote themselves completely to knowing and obeying his Word. The Essenes did this, and John the Baptist went into the same desert to call Israel to repentance and righteous living. So consider the examples of righteous people who have gone before you and learn from them how to walk God's path and prepare his way — that highway through the desert.

1. God chose Abraham to walk in his path and father a people who would prepare the way of the Lord. (See Genesis 18:18 – 19.)

   a. How was Abraham to accomplish this?

   b. Do you think the way Abraham walked God's path is how God wants his people to prepare his way today? Why or why not?

2. When the Israelites were in the desert, what did God command them to do in order to prepare his way? (See Deuteronomy 5:32 – 33; 10:12 – 13.)

3. What instructions did David give to Solomon regarding how to walk in God's path? (See 1 Kings 2:1 – 4; 3:10 – 14.)

What indicates that at least at the beginning of his reign, Solomon sought to walk in God's path as Abraham had? (See 1 Kings 3:10 – 11.)

In what sense did God "walk" with Solomon, and how was Solomon's walk preparing the way for the Lord? (See 1 Kings 3:12 – 14, 28.)

4. What does Psalm 15 teach you about how to walk God's path in daily life?

In what ways are these instructions a practical expression of how Abraham kept God's path?

What do you think would happen if God's people today began to seriously prepare his path in this manner?

5. The restoration of God's people, preparing the way of the Lord, and descriptions of messianic hope are recurring themes in the prophet Isaiah's writings. They provided exciting hope for the Jewish people during the time of Jesus when they longed to be delivered from Rome's oppressive rule. Read Isaiah 40:3 – 5; 57:13 – 19; 62:10 – 12. According to these prophecies:

   a. What kind of people will prepare the way of the Lord?

   b. What will God do to restore his presence in the lives of his people?

   c. What will happen when the way of the Lord is prepared?

d. What do you think God's faithful people, who knew these prophecies well, expected to see happen when John appeared in the desert and began proclaiming a message of repentance and faithful obedience?

6. As prophesied by Isaiah (Isaiah 40:3 – 5) and Malachi (Malachi 3:1), John the Baptist came to "prepare the way" for the Messiah.

a. What did John do to prepare the way, and what did the people do to prepare the way? (See Matthew 3:1 - 9; Mark 1:1 - 4.)

b. The priest Zechariah, John's father, knew that God had given his son the task of preparing the way for the Lord by preparing his people for his coming. How did John prepare the people to prepare the way for the Lord, and what would be the result in their lives? (See Luke 1:76 - 79.)

THINK ABOUT IT
A Highway for Our God

Isaiah 40:3–5 issues an inspiring call for God's people to make a way—a "highway" for him—in the desert. That's a daunting task. Note the rugged high mountains and deep valley in the photo of the Judea Wilderness. Obviously it would take great commitment to prepare such a highway. How

A TYPICAL *DEREKH* (PATH) IN THE WILDERNESS OF JUDEA

much effort are you willing to expend in order to repent of your sins, receive God's forgiveness, and dedicate yourself to walk in God's path by obeying his Word?

Reflection

Jesus has come, and he will come again, so we should not be deaf to Isaiah's plea to prepare the way of the Lord. God still calls his people to prepare his way by faithfully and obediently "walking" in his path. The paths of righteous people are clearly linked to the way of the Lord. Psalm 85:13 reads, "Righteousness goes before him and prepares the way for his steps." What a privilege we have to walk in his path of righteousness — to wear it down, smooth it out, build it up — knowing that our steps of obedience create a great highway for the feet of our coming Lord and Savior.

How passionately do you want to walk in God's path of righteousness? Do you know how to do it?

How eagerly do you study the Bible to learn how to prepare the way of the Lord?

How faithfully do you remind yourself to choose God's path rather than your own path?

As you seek to walk God's path and prepare his way in your world, choose every day to specifically:

- Repent from disobedience and unfaithfulness to God.
- Seek forgiveness through the sacrifice of Jesus the Messiah.
- Recommit to studying and obeying God's Word.
- Join in a caring community to encourage one another and to share with each other as needs arise.
- Live in a godly (righteous) way.
- Look for the presence of the Holy Spirit of God to flow through the community.

What does it mean to you that God raised up an entire people — from Abraham to the Jewish people of Jesus' day — to prepare the way for Messiah's coming?

Who do you think God wants to raise up to prepare the way for his second coming?

What role might your walk in God's path play in preparing his way and making his presence known in your family, your faith community, your school or workplace, and beyond?

Day Four | Stones and Rocks on the Path

The Very Words of God

> *God is our refuge and strength,*
> *an ever-present help in trouble.*
> *Therefore we will not fear ...*
> *The LORD Almighty is with us;*
> *the God of Jacob is our fortress.*
>
> *Psalm 46:1 – 2, 7*

Bible Discovery

When Stones Make Our Path Difficult

In the biblical world, most people traveled from place to place on foot. Some of the paths they walked were wide and well worn, such as the trade routes on which people had traveled for centuries. Other paths were well traveled but narrow and dangerous, twisting and turning up steep mountainsides. Still others were difficult to follow. And on nearly every path a traveler would encounter rocks and stones. In some places there wasn't much to walk on other than stones!

A person doesn't have to walk very far in the lands of the Bible, particularly in the deserts, to realize that if "walking a path" symbolized a person's passage through life, it wasn't going to be easy. If walking through the desert is a picture of the life God's people are called to live — the path they are to walk — it will be very difficult at times. The stones we encounter on our life's path may make our way dangerous, painful, and seemingly impossible. They may cause us to stumble and suffer injury. But God never abandons us when we walk in his path. No matter how rough the path is, he remains with us.

WHEN THE STONES UNDER OUR FEET CAUSE US TO STUMBLE, AND THE ROCKS AHEAD SEEM INSURMOUNTABLE, GOD IS WITH US.

1. Some "stones" that we may encounter on our life's path are caused by other people or natural forces. As you consider each of the following examples, notice how difficult or painful the trouble was and think of times when you have encountered similar stones on your life's path.

    Abraham (Genesis 12:1 – 7, 10)

    Hezekiah (2 Kings 20:1 – 3)

    Job (Job 1:13 – 20)

Widow (1 Kings 17:12 – 18)

Joseph (Genesis 37:14 – 28)

2. Sometimes the stones that cause us to stumble on life's path are there because we've stepped — even for a short time — off God's good path. We may stumble over the enticement of immorality or the seduction of wealth, fame, or power. The path of wickedness is littered with stumbling stones, some of which God puts in our path to get our attention so we will not continue to pursue our own path. As you consider the following examples, notice the stones that caused people to stumble and how they responded to their fall. Think of how you have responded when you have encountered stumbling stones on your life's path.

David (2 Samuel 11:1 – 17, 27; 12:13 – 18)

Absalom (2 Samuel 15:1 – 12; 17:1 – 4; 18:9 – 18)

Manasseh (2 Chronicles 33:1 – 13)

Nebuchadnezzar (Daniel 4:24 – 37)

3. What happens when people cling to the path of rebellion and refuse to walk in God's path? (See Proverbs 4:18 – 19; Jeremiah 18:15; Hosea 14:9; Romans 9:30 – 33.)

4. When those who faithfully walk God's path encounter stones, God promises not to forsake them. How did the biblical writers describe the ways by which God manifests his loving presence to the righteous when they face trouble? (See Psalm 34:17 – 22; Isaiah 40:28 – 31.)

Which images or descriptions of God's presence and provision encourage you to turn to him when you need help on life's path?

5. Although those who encounter stones while walking God's path still face struggle, loss, and pain, what attitudes of praise, gratitude, and hope does God's loving presence inspire? (See Psalms 56:10 – 13; 119:161 – 168; Proverbs 3:21 – 26.)

In what ways do these passages give you peace, hope, and confidence as you deal with the stones on your life's path?

Reflection

Metaphorically speaking, life will throw stones — and sometimes nasty boulders — across our path. But if we walk in God's path and choose him as our dwelling place and refuge, we have nothing to fear when our path becomes rocky. Psalm 91 beautifully portrays God's presence and provision during such times. Read it, meditate on it, and remember whose path you walk. Then look at the rocky portions of your life's path — past and present — and remember how God has been with you.

> Which small stones have you faced on God's path, and in what way(s) have they made life difficult but not so difficult that you could not keep walking?

> Which larger stones have hurt enough that you needed to stop and regain your strength before moving forward?

> Which large rocks of extended pain and struggle have you faced — diseases, shattered relationships, alienation from children, job loss, economic hardships — that have stopped you in your tracks?

> Which boulders have been so overwhelming that you could not see the path beyond them?

Memorize

If you make the Most High your dwelling —
  even the L̲ORD, who is my refuge —
then no harm will befall you,
  no disaster will come near your tent.
For he will command his angels concerning you
  to guard you in all your ways;
they will lift you up in their hands,
  so that you will not strike your foot against a stone.
You will tread upon the lion and the cobra;
  you will trample the great lion and the serpent.
"Because he loves me," says the L̲ORD, "I will rescue him;
  I will protect him, for he acknowledges my name.
He will call upon me, and I will answer him;
  I will be with him in trouble,
  I will deliver him and honor him.
With long life will I satisfy him
  and show him my salvation."

Psalm 91:9 – 16

Day Five | Honey in the Rock

The Very Words of God

"If my people would but listen to me,
  if Israel would follow my ways . . .
you would be fed with the finest of wheat;
  with honey from the rock I would satisfy you."

Psalm 81:13, 16

Bible Discovery

Taste that the Lord Is Good!

The biblical writers often portray God and his interaction with his
people figuratively, using familiar images from their world. They
describe God, for example, as bread and living water, shade and the
refuge of solid rock. And they describe God's people experiencing

him through their senses — hearing, seeing, touching, and even tasting. Thus the psalmist says, "Taste and see that the LORD is good" (Psalm 34:8). Although the biblical writers never attribute a particular taste to God, a number of passages connect God and his presence to a delicacy the Jewish people knew and loved: honey.

1. The Hebrew people spent four centuries in Egypt, and at the time of their deliverance many of them no longer knew their God. What did they experience as they walked the desert path that caused them to rediscover their God and learn to trust and obey him? (See Deuteronomy 8:2 – 3; 32:10 – 13.)

2. During their desert journey, the Israelites craved the food of Egypt, and God responded by raining down "bread from heaven" to satisfy them. What did the manna taste like, and in what sense did it give them a taste of God? (See Exodus 16:1 – 4, 31, 35.)

3. Who did Jesus say was the source of the bread of heaven the Israelites received in the desert? (See John 6:30 – 35.)

    How did Jesus use God's provision of manna to teach about himself?

In what sense did Jesus, like the manna God provided in the desert, give us a taste of God?

4. Read Psalms 19:9 – 11; 119:97 – 103; Ezekiel 3:1 – 3. What is compared to honey in these passages?

In what sense do God's words and law give us a taste of God?

5. Which metaphor does Proverbs 24:13 – 14 use to describe wisdom, and what are its benefits?

Since wisdom comes from God, in what sense does it also give us a taste of God?

6. When God brought Israel out of Egypt, what did he want them to do, and what did he want to do for them? (See Psalm 81:10, 13, 16.)

Do you think God wants his people to experience this kind of relationship with him today? Why or why not?

Reflection

When we choose to follow God and walk obediently in his path, we will experience his blessings. We will also encounter stones on our path. Again and again the Bible records that during Israel's difficult times in the desert, when they faced stones on the path, they also tasted the "sweetness" of God and his deliverance. In the midst of pain and struggle, he provided the "honey" of manna from heaven, water from rock, deliverance from enemies, healing ...

Reflect on your life's path. No doubt you too have encountered "stones," "rocks," and possibly "boulders."

In what ways has God been present on your path and given you a taste of honey through caring people, healing and restoration, or just enough of himself to keep walking another moment or day?

How "sweet" was his provision to you at the time, and is it still as sweet in your memory?

Although we might prefer that God provide for us by removing the stones from our path so that our "ankles do not turn" (2 Samuel 22:37) and we avoid the pain and hardship of life's path, why do you think he often allows stones on our path and chooses to provide honey from the rock or manna just for one day at a time?

What happens in your relationship with God when you find the honey he has provided in a rock of struggle?

What happens in your relationship with God when you go out every day to gather the sweet manna he has provided to sustain you?

First Peter 2:3 speaks of maturing in our salvation and having "tasted that the Lord is good." What do you have to share with other people about your God and his sweet presence on a rocky path?

Memorize

Taste and see that the LORD is good;
    blessed is the man who takes refuge in him.
Fear the LORD, you his saints,
    for those who fear him lack nothing.
The lions may grow weak and hungry,
    but those who seek the LORD lack no good thing.

Psalm 34:8 – 10

EARS TO HEAR

"The LORD is my shepherd." These familiar words from Psalm 23 have brought hope and encouragement into the lives of God's people for more than three thousand years. But even greater meanings emerge when this phrase is understood in the context of the way Middle Eastern shepherds lead and care for their flocks.

The Israelites were desert people and raised sheep and goats that could survive on the meager grass and water found there. For both the shepherd and the flock, life in the rugged terrain and harsh climate of the desert was difficult. Flocks were rarely fenced in, so they were totally dependent on their shepherds to provide shelter, protection, and enough daily pasture and water to survive. The flock's helpless dependence on the shepherd's leading and provision became an appropriate metaphor for the relationship between God and his people. Like sheep in the desert, the Israelites learned to depend totally on God to provide "just enough" food, water, and protection to survive each day.

The shepherd was both the flock's leader and constant companion. As protector, the shepherd carried a "rod" — a clublike weapon — and a "staff" to drive away predators. Yet the shepherd treated the sheep gently, anticipating their every need and even carrying those that became weak or injured. As provider, the shepherd called to the flock, leading it to water and fresh pasture by voice. Shepherds in biblical times were so closely linked to their flock that they could separate it from larger flocks simply by calling to their animals. The sheep, in turn, responded only to the voice of their particular shepherd.

What an amazing picture of the kind of relationship God desires to have with his people! God led his people out of Egypt and into the desert in order to show them that he was their Shepherd who cared deeply for them and would provide for all their needs. As their Shepherd, he lovingly taught them to listen to his voice, obey his words, and follow wherever he led.

To better understand the metaphor of God as Shepherd of his people, we must remember that in the Middle East flocks are not found in the lush landscape of belly-deep alfalfa where they might survive on their own. Rather, they are found in the barren desert wilderness where the presence of a good shepherd can mean the difference between life and death. So it is with us.

God, our Shepherd, meets us in the desert too. He is committed to lead and protect us during our desert experiences — the painful times of significant suffering and struggle in our lives. As scary and difficult as these deserts may be, they provide the opportunity for us to learn to follow his voice and discover that we can trust and depend on him completely. Through his Word, God invites each of us to experience him as our compassionate Shepherd who loves us, cares for us, and faithfully provides just what we need for each day — and sometimes much more.

Opening Thoughts (3 minutes)

The Very Words of God

> He brought his people out like a flock;
> > he led them like sheep through the desert.
> He guided them safely, so they were unafraid.

Psalm 78:52 – 53

Think About It

Every culture values some things more highly than others and perceives the world through that lens. One culture, for example, may value physical beauty or artistry and view the world according to what they see. Another may value athletic prowess or economic power and evaluate the world according to what they can achieve.

What do you think your culture values most highly, and to what extent do those values influence your beliefs and choices and affect what you are able to hear, see, and understand?

DVD Notes (23 minutes)

Why the desert?

Desert wilderness—the land of the shepherd

Led by the shepherd's voice

The "green" pastures of the wilderness

Trusting God to provide just enough

DVD Discussion (7 minutes)

1. On the map on page 237, locate Goshen in the Nile delta of
   Lower Egypt. Then locate the vast desert regions of the Sinai
   Peninsula, Judea Wilderness, and Negev. On the inset map,
   locate the Negev and Judea Wilderness, then the Desert of
   Zin, Desert of Maon, Desert of Ziph.

   Imagine that you had lived as a Hebrew in ancient Egypt with
   its sophisticated culture, planned cities, elaborate and color-
   ful temples, and lush, fertile farmlands. When God uprooted
   you to lead you into the vast desert wastelands on your way
   toward the "green pastures" of the Promised Land, would he
   have captured your full attention? Why or why not?

   In what ways do you see that radical desert experience chang-
   ing your spiritual perception from what you can see with your
   eyes to that of understanding God through your ears?

Think about how you perceive God today. How might God get your attention so that you could learn to hear him, know him, and obey him better than you do now?

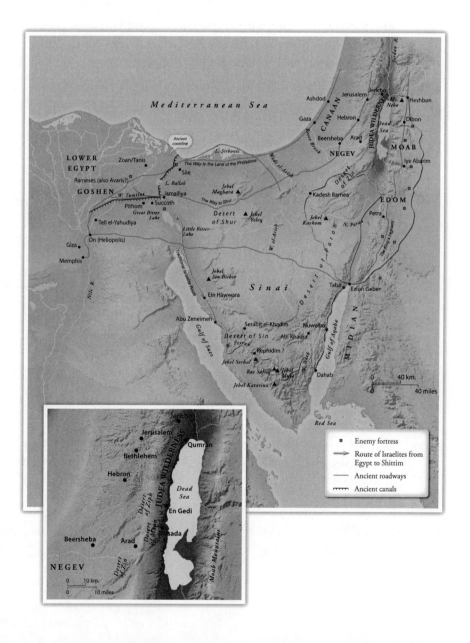

2. What surprised you about the "green pastures" of Israel, and how do they differ from what you expected?

    In what ways do these green pastures cause you to rethink your view of what God, our Shepherd, provides for us and what it means for us to depend on him daily?

3. How did seeing what the "straight path" or "paths of righteousness" actually look like help you to better understand what it means to be led on them?

    What did you learn about the constant, watchful care of the shepherd who leads the flock on paths of righteousness?

    If you are a sheep, how important is it for you to always listen for the Shepherd's voice and promptly follow wherever it leads? What might happen if you don't?

4. What else did you learn through the video that amazed you or gave you a new understanding of God and the relationship he desires to have with you?

5. As you think about the whole picture of God being our Good Shepherd that you have just seen, to what extent can you now hear his voice just a little bit better? Follow him a little closer?

Small Group Bible Discovery and Discussion (20 minutes)

The Desert: Where the Flock Learns to Trust the Shepherd

What do you picture when you think of the biblical metaphor of God as shepherd and his people as sheep?[1] Many of us think immediately of the protection, comfort, and contentment God provides for those who follow him. An image of a relaxing vacation at a pristine lake surrounded by green, grassy meadows may come to mind. Although God can (and does) provide abundantly for his people, we tend to overlook the fact that often he provides for us when we're facing difficult circumstances in the desert. The sun is still hot, our path is still steep, but God gives us just enough to keep us going.

The "just-enough" blessings shape and mold God's people into a trusting community that loves him and depends on him to provide for its every need. Consider the trust and obedience the Israelites learned when God provided just enough manna for each day and any remaining manna spoiled (except the extra Sabbath ration). Even when his people settled in the Promised Land, each family received just enough land to live contentedly in a relationship of trust, obedience, and dependence on him. God still desires to shape and mold those who follow him into a people who trust him fully and obey him faithfully. So he leads us, like sheep, into the "desert" where we learn to love him as our Shepherd.

1. During biblical times, in what kinds of locations did shepherds typically tend their sheep? (See Genesis 13:1 – 6; Exodus 3:1; 1 Samuel 25:1 – 2; Jeremiah 23:10.)

DID YOU KNOW?
Flocks in the Desert

In the ancient Middle East, most shepherds lived in tents and tended their animals in the barren desert. To use fertile land as pasture for flocks and herds would have made it difficult for God's people to produce enough olives, grain, figs, and grapes to survive. Flocks occasionally grazed in cultivated areas during times of political unrest. They also entered the fields and ate the remaining stubble after the grain harvest. So when the Bible describes God and his people as a shepherd and his flock, the original readers — as Middle Eastern readers do today — assumed that the flock was in the desert.

In what ways do you think the nature of these lands would tend to shape the relationship between sheep and shepherd, and what might you expect that relationship to look like?

NOTE: Refer to the map on page 237 to locate these deserts.

2. What does Isaiah 49:8 – 10, 13 reveal about how passionately God desires to care and provide for his people?

Where would God's people be if they needed this kind of care?

In what ways does this passage describe the way a shepherd cares for a flock?

How descriptive is this passage of the kind of care people today need in their "deserts"?

3. For what specific purposes did God, through Moses, lead his people into the desert? (See Exodus 15:22 - 26; Deuteronomy 8:1 - 3.)

Do you think God allows his people to endure painful desert experiences for the same purposes today? If not, why not? If so, how might this change the way we view and respond to our desert experiences?

4. While the Israelites were in the desert, in what ways was God like a shepherd to them?

Text	The Way God Was Like a Shepherd
Ex. 13:20–22	
Ex. 14:19–20	
Ex. 16:4–5, 13–15	
Ex. 17:1–7	
Ex. 23:20–22	
Ps. 78:51–55	
Isa. 40:11	

5. Why is the condition of the hearts of God's people so impor-
    tant to him? (See Psalm 95:6 – 10.)

    What happens when the members of the flock harden their
    hearts to the shepherd's voice?

6. When Israel (Jacob) was very old and had been reunited
    with his son Joseph in Egypt, he had the opportunity to
    bless his grandsons. What did he say about who God had
    been in his life and what God had done for him? (See Gen-
    esis 48:10 – 16.)

    What testimony of who God has been in your life and what
    he has done for you do you want to leave for future genera-
    tions?

    How much time might you need to spend in the desert in
    order to become a "sheep" that shares such an intimate and
    rewarding relationship with the Shepherd?

Faith Lesson (6 minutes)

One way to understand the relationship between shepherd and sheep in the desert is to realize that all people experience times of "desert" — pain, illness, rejection, loss, grief, struggle, and heartache. That is the nature of living in a sinful, broken world. But it is also the nature of God, our Shepherd, to lead, provide for, and care for his flock. In fact, some of the most experienced desert travelers who have gone before us would say that even during their most difficult times in the desert, the Lord provided so that *they lacked nothing*!

1. In his final speech to the Israelites before they left the desert, Moses said, "The Lord your God has blessed you ... has watched over your journey through this vast desert. These forty years the Lord your God has been with you, and you have not lacked anything" (Deuteronomy 2:7). David said, "The Lord is my shepherd, I lack nothing" (Psalm 23:1 TNIV).

    a. How do you think Moses could say this when God's people had been living in tents in the desert, running out of water, and gathering manna daily instead of living in houses in the Promised Land where they could grow wheat, grapes, olives, pomegranates, and figs?

    b. How do you think David could say this when he had been running for his life in the scorching heat of the Judea Wilderness and hiding in caves when he knew that a palace and the life of a king awaited him?

    c. What would you say about God's provision for you during your desert experiences?

2. Many of us are at least a little like the man Jesus spoke of who had more than he needed for the day and stored up enough food for many years (Luke 12:16–21).

    a. How do you think some time in the desert might have helped him regain an attitude of trust and dependence on God for what he needed each day?

    b. To what extent do you believe that God will "shepherd" you well — whether you are in fruitful farmland or the barren desert — and provide enough to satisfy your needs one day at a time?

3. When the Lord is your Shepherd (meaning that you are part of his flock, listening for his voice and obeying his words), what do you think it means that you will lack nothing?

What is the difference between having everything you want as opposed to everything you need?

Who determines what the sheep need — the Shepherd or the sheep? What does that mean for you and your trust in the Shepherd?

Closing (1 minute)

Read Psalm 23 aloud, "The LORD is my shepherd, I shall not be in want. He makes me lie down in green pastures, he leads me beside quiet waters, he restores my soul. He guides me in paths of righteousness for his name's sake. Even though I walk through the valley of the shadow of death, I will fear no evil, for you are with me; your rod and your staff, they comfort me. You prepare a table before me in the presence of my enemies. You anoint my head with oil; my cup overflows. Surely goodness and love will follow me all the days of my life, and I will dwell in the house of the LORD forever."

Then pray, thanking God for being your Shepherd. Ask him to help you to trust him completely and teach you how to listen for his voice and follow him faithfully just as a sheep follows its shepherd.

Memorize

> *The LORD is my shepherd, I shall not be in want.*
> *He makes me lie down in green pastures,*
> *he leads me beside quiet waters,*
> *he restores my soul.*
> *He guides me in paths of righteousness*
> *for his name's sake.*
> *Even though I walk*
> *through the valley of the shadow of death,*
> *I will fear no evil,*
> *for you are with me;*
> *your rod and your staff,*
> *they comfort me.*

You prepare a table before me
in the presence of my enemies.
You anoint my head with oil;
my cup overflows.
Surely goodness and love will follow me
all the days of my life,
and I will dwell in the house of the LORD
forever.

Psalm 23

Walking with God through Our Deserts

In-Depth Personal Study Sessions

Day One | The Way to Green Pastures

The Very Words of God

> *I am always with you;*
> > *you hold me by my right hand.*
> *You guide me with your counsel,*
> > *and afterward you will take me into glory.*
> *Whom have I in heaven but you?*
> > *And earth has nothing I desire besides you.*
> *My flesh and my heart may fail,*
> > *but God is the strength of my heart*
> > *and my portion forever.*
> *Those who are far from you will perish;*
> > *you destroy all who are unfaithful to you.*
> *But as for me, it is good to be near God.*
> > *I have made the Sovereign LORD my refuge;*
> > *I will tell of all your deeds.*

Psalm 73:23 – 28

Bible Discovery

Stay Close to the Shepherd

When people visit Bible lands for the first time, they discover that things are quite different (sometimes startlingly so) from what they had imagined. "The Sea of Galilee is so much smaller (or so much bigger)," they say. Or, "Jerusalem and Bethlehem are so close together." Or, "There is so much desert and the mountains are so steep." Almost all first-time visitors are most surprised by the "green pastures," the barren desert hills with sparse tufts of grass where shepherds[2] live with their herds and flocks.

**IT LACKS BELLY-HIGH GRASS, BUT THIS DESERT PASTURE HAS A
DISTINCTIVE GREENISH TINT AFTER THE WINTER RAINS.**

In the desert pasture setting, God's provision for his sheep has
implications that we easily miss if we view them through the lens of
rich pasturelands of tall grass that are found in other regions of the
world. The shepherd wants the sheep to be safe, fed, and watered.
In desert pastures where there is constant danger, little water, and
sparse grass, the sheep can't be allowed to wander aimlessly. They
must stay close to the shepherd who leads them to what they need.
It is the same for us. In order for us to be sensitive to our Shepherd's
guiding presence and caring provision during our desert experiences, we must remain very close to him.

1. According to the psalmist, how does a person find "green
    pastures" and "quiet waters"? (See Psalm 23:1 – 2.)

How do you think you would fare if you walked into the Negev or Judea Wilderness on your own seeking green pastures and quiet waters?

How successful are you in finding the strength and refreshment you need — the green pastures and quiet waters of the wilderness — when you are going through desert experiences?

2. Many of the psalms are personal expressions of one's relationship with God. What do you learn from the following psalms about the ways a person can stay close to God in the desert? (See Psalms 31:1 - 3, 14 - 15; 119:10 - 16; 143:8 - 10.)

3. The apostle Paul was intent on walking as Jesus did, or to put it in language we typically use, living in close fellowship with God. How closely did he pursue God — his Shepherd? (See Philippians 1:20 - 21; 3:12 - 14.)

What deserts had Paul experienced, and what need do you think he had for the loving care, protection, and provision of the Shepherd? (See 2 Corinthians 11:24 – 28.)

In Philippians 4:12 – 13, what evidence do you see that Paul was content with the Shepherd's provision for his life, that he was, in effect, feeding in green pastures and resting by quiet waters?

4. A close relationship with God, our Shepherd, doesn't happen automatically. We have to want it, and we have to work at it. God led the Israelites through the desert for forty years so that they would learn to draw close to him, listen to him, and live by every word that came from his mouth! What can we do to help nurture our relationship with our Shepherd and remain close to him? As you read each passage below and on page 252, consider carefully how you can apply it in your life.

    Deuteronomy 6:4 – 9; Matthew 22:37 – 39

    John 14:15

    2 Timothy 3:14 – 17

Hebrews 10:22 – 25

1 John 1:9 – 10

1 John 2:3 – 6

DID YOU KNOW?

Tufts of Grass

Sometimes it looks as if there's nothing other than rocks to eat in Israel's desert pastures! There's a good reason for that. The tufts of grass that grow in the desert pastures usually grow from underneath or between the rocks.

Although very little rain falls on desert pastures, the moisture is retained in the heavy soil. The soil under the stones is protected from the burning sun, so it remains moist well into the dry

A TUFT OF GRASS THRIVES IN A ROCKY DESERT PASTURE.

season. In addition, moisture from breezes off the Mediterranean Sea condenses on the warm rocks and drips onto the soil. It's not much, but it is

SHEEP SURVIVE A MOUTHFUL AT A TIME ON THE SPARSE DESERT PASTURES.

enough for small tufts of grass to grow around the rocks and provide pasture for flocks.

Sheep in the desert pastures need a shepherd to lead them. There is sufficient grass, but it is sparse. Not every hillside receives rain or is exposed to moisture-laden sea breezes. Sheep left on their own will wander searching for grass and eventually die. Staying close to their shepherd is a matter of life and death for them.

Reflection

The reality of life in desert pastures makes it easier to understand how much the sheep need a shepherd and how essential it is for them to stay close to their shepherd. In order to experience the green pastures God has for us in our deserts, it's important that we follow him closely too. Our natural tendency is to choose our own path and to stockpile resources for the future so that we can live independently of our Shepherd. But that's not God's best for us.

God desires that the sheep of his flock trust him and depend on him completely. He will faithfully provide green pastures for us, just as he provided manna in the desert for forty years, but we need to stay close enough to hear his voice and follow him. Then we will receive at least enough to satisfy our needs — one mouthful at a time — today, tomorrow, and always.

In which circumstances do you find it easier and in which circumstances do you find it more difficult to stay in close relationship with God and trust him to meet your needs?

In what ways has living in a culture that values consumption of far more than we need influenced your perception of your needs (as opposed to your wants)?

What happens to your sense of dependence on God for your daily needs when you have more than you need?

How might an economic downturn — even a depression — lead you to draw closer to God and test the depth of your trust in his provision?

If you have experienced times when you have not been able to provide for yourself, where did you turn for help and what sustained you?

What happened to your sense of dependence on God for your every need during that time, and how does the memory of that time affect you today?

How eagerly did you look for God and seek to follow him during that time, and how does the memory of that time affect your relationship with him today?

How aware were you at the time of God's "mouthful-by-mouthful" provision, and did you believe it was enough? Why or why not?

How might you want your relationship with God to be different if you face times of extreme need in the future?

Psalm 73:23 – 28 provides a beautiful picture of what it is like to remain close to God and receive his provision. Memorize it and live it.

Memorize

I am always with you;
*   you hold me by my right hand.*
You guide me with your counsel,
*   and afterward you will take me into glory.*
Whom have I in heaven but you?
*   And earth has nothing I desire besides you.*
My flesh and my heart may fail,
*   but God is the strength of my heart*
*   and my portion forever.*
Those who are far from you will perish;
*   you destroy all who are unfaithful to you.*
But as for me, it is good to be near God.
*   I have made the Sovereign Lord my refuge;*
*   I will tell of all your deeds.*

Psalm 73:23 – 28

Day Two | The Desert: Land of God's Word

The Very Words of God

Remember how the Lord your God led you all the way in the desert
these forty years, to humble you and to test you in order to know what
was in your heart, whether or not you would keep his commands ...
to teach you that man does not live on bread alone but on every word
that comes from the mouth of the Lord.

Deuteronomy 8:2 – 3

Bible Discovery

Listen to Your Shepherd's Voice

Shepherds in the Middle East exercise total control over their sheep not by driving the sheep or using dogs to herd them, but by their voice. It is amazing to hear the singsong voices of shepherd girls as they call to their sheep. Gently speaking meaningful words and sounds to their flocks, they lead their sheep across the hillsides.

Just as shepherds train their flocks to respond to their voice so they can lead the animals to the safety, rest, and nourishment of the next pasture the shepherd has selected for them, God trained Israel to respond to every word that came from his mouth. In order to teach his people to follow him as their Shepherd, he led them into harsh deserts where shepherds typically lived. There, in the midst of their daily struggles, he molded them into a flock that obediently followed his voice.

As Shepherd of his people today, God may lead us into the deserts of life too. Sometimes we can hear his voice only in our deserts — in the silence of hard times. As we struggle through the pain of broken relationships, sickness, betrayal, failure, or death, God leads us by his voice, his words. We may hear him speak through the words of his inspired book, the Bible. We may hear his voice through the lives of other people who follow him and the testimony of his creation around us. Although hearing God's voice may come through struggle — like honey from a rock — hearing and following it leads us to the green pastures of his daily care and provision.

1. After Moses completed writing the law and the priests put it into the ark of the covenant, what command did God give concerning what all of Israel must do with his words? (See Deuteronomy 31:9 – 13.)

   Why do you think God commanded that his people *hear,* not just *read,* all of his words (the Torah was all they had when this command was given)? What might he have wanted his people to hear in his words?

When was the last time you *heard* all of God's words? (Or more than a few verses?)

If you knew God well enough and knew his words well enough that you could, in a sense, hear his voice in his words, how might your relationship with him change?

2. What does the Bible tell us about the words of God our Shepherd? (See Psalms 18:30; 33:4; 119:89, 105.)

How would such words, if we listen to them and obey them, help us to stay on the right path in the desert?

3. When God's people hear his voice, what does he want them to do regarding the words he speaks? (See Exodus 15:26; Deuteronomy 4:12 - 14; 5:4 - 22; 1 Samuel 15:22 - 23; Haggai 1:12 - 13.)

How is this like the way a shepherd leads sheep through the desert?

What are the benefits for sheep that obey God's voice, and what happens when they refuse to obey it?

4. Jesus identified himself as a shepherd on several occasions, none more directly than in John 10:1 – 16. What did Jesus say about how his sheep would know him and respond to his leading?

DATA FILE

God's Words in the Desert

The Torah books, set in the desert, refer to God's *words* more than fifty times. The inspired writer recorded them all to ensure that they would remain the formative influence on God's people he desired. God even commanded that every seven years all Israel must assemble to hear his words so they too would revere him and follow his path. In the desert's silence, the spoken word of God would be heard, and God used that opportunity to the fullest.

In classic Eastern fashion, the inspired writer of the Torah linked *word* and *desert* by using words having the same root. The Hebrew word translated "word," *dabar*, has the letters *dbr* (רבד) and also can be translated "response," "promise," "answer," or "commandment." *Dabar* is also the root

continued on next page . . .

word for *midbar,* which means "desert" — arid places where there is just enough pasture for flocks. These word links strengthen the message God chose to speak to his people in the desert.

For example, God led Israel, his flock, into the desert (*midbar*) to instruct (*dabbret*) them in the Ten Commandments (Hebrew: ten words [*debar*]) and to teach them to live on every word (*dabar*) that came from his mouth. The Hebrew word translated "pasture," *dober,* is also based on the root *dbr* and is drawn from the fact that the shepherd (Hebrew root noun for "desert," *dabar,* also means "leader" or "shepherd") typically lived in the desert rather than in fertile, farmed areas. So God led his flock into the desert (*midbar*) pasture (*dober*) where he spoke (*dibber*) so Israel would receive and learn his words (*dabar*).[3] What new insights do you have into how much God wanted his words to be heard, understood, remembered, and obeyed in the context of the desert?

Reflection

Following my heart attack and subsequent bypass surgery a few years ago, I (Ray) had many hours of inactivity as I recovered. I would sit in an easy chair looking out the window into the beautiful woods around my home and sense the presence and encouragement of God in my struggle. The Bible became even more vivid and real as I read it. I heard God speak to me as I had never heard him before.

Later, when I resumed my active life, I often discovered that God had "talked" to me during my recovery in ways I had not even recognized. Bible passages took on new or added meaning as I realized how God had faithfully kept his word while I was in that desert. I do not want to return to that experience, but during that time I learned to listen for and follow God's voice, and for that I am grateful.

Jesus is looking for "sheep" who not only know his teachings, but know their Shepherd's voice and follow (obey) him. How would you describe your knowledge of Jesus?

Do you listen for his voice? Know his voice? Follow his voice by obeying his words? Can you truly say that he is your Shepherd?

What insights do you gain from the fact that God led his people into the silence of the desert in order to teach them to hear and obey his words?

What might he need to do in order to create enough silence in your life that you can hear his voice?

When in your life have you heard God's voice and words most clearly?

What did you learn during that time about how to listen for his voice that helps you to follow him today?

Jesus is our Shepherd, and because shepherds typically live in the desert with their flocks, those who follow him might expect to spend some time in the desert as well. How highly do you value your relationship with your Shepherd?

What hard work and struggle are you willing to endure in order to know and hear his voice?

How far are you willing to follow him over rocky hillsides and through wadis to hear his words and learn to obey them?

Memorize

"You do not believe because you are not my sheep. My sheep listen to my voice; I know them, and they follow me. I give them eternal life, and they shall never perish; no one can snatch them out of my hand."

John 10:26 – 28

Day Three | God Our Shepherd Provides

The Very Words of God

See, the Sovereign LORD comes with power,
*   and his arm rules for him....*
He tends his flock like a shepherd:
*   He gathers the lambs in his arms*
and carries them close to his heart;
*   he gently leads those that have young.*

Isaiah 40:10 – 11

Bible Discovery

Our Compassionate Provider

In deserts of the Middle East, sheep are helpless to find food, water, and shelter. They easily lose their way and have no defenses against predators. Without a shepherd, they do not survive for long. In this context, the Bible portrays the shepherd as a caring, compassionate, protective provider who chooses safe paths where the flock will enjoy adequate pasture and good water. Scripture especially uses the shepherd metaphor to describe the character and work of the Messiah — God in flesh — who would come to seek and to save God's flock.

1. The Middle Eastern shepherd provides a beautiful metaphor of God's constant, loving care for his people. David, the writer of Psalm 23, was such a shepherd. Read thoughtfully Psalm 23:1 - 4, which describes a broad view of how a shepherd provides for the flock.

   Then read Isaiah 40:11, Jeremiah 23:1 - 4, and Ezekiel 34:1 - 16, and list on the chart below all of the ways our Lord as Shepherd cares and provides for his flock. (Note that some of what the Good Shepherd does is presented in light of what bad shepherds do and do not do.)

   Next write down how the Good Shepherd — whether through everyday provision or dramatic intervention — has cared for you in similar ways.

Psalm 23	How Our Shepherd Cares and Provides	How God Has Provided for Me
Pasture and Water		
Restoration		
Guidance		

continued on next page . . .

Psalm 23	How Our Shepherd Cares and Provides	How God Has Provided for Me
Protection		
Comfort		

2. In light of the fact that those who follow Jesus (who walk as he walked) become part of God's flock and receive the Shepherd's loving, compassionate care, what is significant about what Jesus said to his disciples in Matthew 6:31 – 34 and 28:19 – 20?

Does any sheep under the Shepherd's care need to worry about what to eat or drink? Why or why not?

How does a sheep seek the Shepherd's kingdom and righteousness?

Does a sheep have to worry about being abandoned by the Shepherd? Why or why not?

3. In what ways do the following verses connect Jesus the Messiah to the shepherd figure of the Hebrew Bible who cares for the needs of the flock? (See Micah 5:2 – 5; Matthew 9:35 – 36; 25:31 – 32; Luke 2:8 – 20; Luke 15:1 – 7; John 10:1 – 16; Hebrews 13:20 – 21.)

Reflection

Jesus the Messiah loves the sheep of his pasture. Our compassionate Savior, he longs to care and provide for each lamb in the flock — so much so that he willingly sacrificed his life on our behalf. He longs to be in intimate relationship with you and promises to meet your needs if you are part of his flock that listens for his voice, follows (obeys) him, and trusts him to lead them on the right paths — the paths of righteousness.

> What does it mean to you that Jesus the Messiah has also come as your Shepherd to surround you with his protection and provision as he calls to you and gently leads you in his ways?

> How does the fact that Jesus has compassion for sheep who had no shepherd encourage you that you are not alone or uncared for when you face the deserts in your life?

As you explored the many ways by which Jesus provides for his flock, which were most encouraging to you?

What care and provision do you most need today, and will you trust him to provide that for you?

How does viewing Matthew 6:31 – 34 in light of the shepherd-sheep metaphor — Jesus being your watchful, providing Shepherd, and you being the sheep who follows his every word — change how you go about seeking God's kingdom and his righteousness?

Day Four | Jesus the Messiah: Our Shepherd King

The Very Words of God

But you, Bethlehem Ephrathah,
though you are small among the clans of Judah,
out of you will come for me
one who will be ruler over Israel,
whose origins are from of old,
from ancient times....
He will stand and shepherd his flock
in the strength of the LORD,
in the majesty of the name of the LORD his God.
And they will live securely, for then his greatness
will reach to the ends of the earth.

Micah 5:2, 4

Bible Discovery

God Comes as Our Sovereign King

Many people recognize the familiar phrase, "The Lord is my shepherd" (Psalm 23:1), as a metaphor for God's compassionate care and provision for his people. Yet we must not overlook another meaning of *shepherd* that also describes God. Ancient shepherds exercised complete and undisputed authority over their flocks. As an expression of the shepherd's love and devotion to the flock, he determined what was in the animals' best interest and led them from one place to the next whether or not the sheep knew where they were going or wanted to go there. The sheep, figuratively speaking, were completely in the shepherd's hands and under his authority. So, if Jesus Christ is indeed your Shepherd, he has absolute power and authority over your life. He is your divine, sovereign King!

1. The Bible especially uses the shepherd metaphor to describe the character and work of the Messiah — God in flesh — who would come to seek and to save God's flock. He would not only care for the flock, but have divine authority to rule God's flock. As you read the following Bible passages, identify the links that present Jesus as the Messiah-King who has been given divine authority over God's flock. Write them down in the chart so you can grasp the whole picture. Remember, these links may be in metaphorical language, so you will have to look for them. There also may be multiple links in some passages.

Text	Jesus as the Messiah-King
Isa. 9:1 – 2, 6 – 7	
Jer. 23:1 – 6	
Dan. 7:13 – 14	

continued on next page . . .

Text	Jesus as the Messiah-King
Micah 5:2, 4; Matt. 2:1–2	
Zech. 9:9; Matt. 21:1–5	
John 1:29	

What new understanding did you gain from these passages about the divine authority of Jesus the Messiah to rule over his followers?

How does this realization change your perception of the importance of listening to the voice of Jesus, obeying his words, and following him wherever he leads?

2. Not only is the authority of the Messiah-King amazing, his kingdom and rule are like no other. Read the following passages and write on the chart the way the Bible describes his kingdom and rule.

Text	Messiah's Kingdom: What Is it Like to Be Under His Rule?
Isa. 9:1–2, 6–7	

Text	Messiah's Kingdom: What Is it Like to Be Under His Rule?
Ezek. 34:20–31	
Micah 5:4–5	
Rev. 7:15–17	

What appreciation do you now have for the heart of God — his impassioned justice, power, and loving care for his flock — and the way he expresses his authority over his flock?

What comfort do you find in the authority of the Good Shepherd, and to what extent does it cause you to want to follow his voice and obey his words?

3. God chose David from among his flock (Israel) to shepherd his people. What kind of shepherd was David? (See Psalm 78:70–72.)

What kind of a "sheep" was David, and how do you think
that influenced how he led God's flock? (See Psalms 25:4 – 5;
86:11; 119:33 – 37; 139:23 – 24.)

4. Ezekiel 34:8 – 12 describes God's response to the neglect of
    his flock by unfaithful shepherds of Israel. What did God say
    he would do for his lost sheep?

    What did Jesus say about his purpose for coming to earth,
    and how does it relate to what God said he would do for his
    lost sheep? (See Luke 19:9 – 10.)

    Who was Jesus claiming to be in this statement, and by
    whose authority did he teach and lead the flock of God?

Reflection

When we choose to follow Jesus and become a member of his
"flock," we put ourselves under his loving care *and* under his
authority as our King. In the metaphor of sheep and shepherd, this
means we are to listen for his voice and obediently follow him wher-

ever he leads. We may still want to go our own way, especially when the way is difficult, but our Shepherd loves us beyond measure and knows what is best for us. No matter how difficult or painful the desert experiences that he leads us into may be, he is always with us, and following his path is the only way that leads us to life — the green pastures and still waters we need.

We live in a culture in which virtually all aspects of authority are being challenged, and our "right" to choose whatever path we want is highly valued. Given that context, how do you respond to Jesus' authority as your divine Shepherd?

How willing are you to trust him to determine what is in your best interest and to lead you there by the path he chooses — even when it leads through a desert?

To what extent do you resist placing yourself completely under his authority and choose to step onto paths of your own choosing?

What struggles have you experienced because you did not acknowledge and submit to Jesus' authority as your Shepherd and King?

When has Jesus shown his divine authority in your life? How did you respond, and where did that path lead?

The Bible repeatedly speaks of God's people rejoicing at the coming of their King. As you have discovered more about following Jesus as both your Shepherd and your King, what causes you to rejoice?

Memorize

Rejoice greatly, O Daughter of Zion!
Shout, Daughter of Jerusalem!
See, your king comes to you,
righteous and having salvation,
gentle and riding on a donkey,
on a colt, the foal of a donkey.

Zechariah 9:9

Day Five | Walking in Paths of Righteousness

The Very Words of God

I long for your salvation, O LORD,
and your law is my delight.
Let me live that I may praise you,
and may your laws sustain me.
I have strayed like a lost sheep.
Seek your servant,
for I have not forgotten your commands.

Psalm 119:174 – 176

Bible Discovery

Our Shepherd Knows the Way

Walking in the deserts of Israel is never easy. The heat and steep, rocky terrain of mountains that never seem to end are exhausting. Hillsides look exactly alike. Deep, narrow valleys make it difficult to see more than a short distance in any direction. Even more confusing are the myriad crisscrossing paths that encircle most hillsides. Called "straight paths" or "paths of righteousness" in the Bible, these paths are created by grazing flocks and their shepherds. No wonder it is easy to lose one's way in these deserts.

Shepherds who live here know the paths well — which ones lead to water, which lead to better pasture, which are dangerous, which are deadends. When it is time to move their flock, shepherds choose the right path to lead their sheep in the direction they must go. Walking ahead on the right path, the shepherds call to their sheep and the sheep respond by following the path that leads to their shepherd. Consider how the Good Shepherd, in a similar way, calls out to us to take the straight path that leads to him and the provision we need.

THE SHEEP FOLLOW THEIR SHEPHERD.

1. What do the following verses reveal about how the sheep
    need a shepherd? (See Psalm 119:174 - 176; Jeremiah 50:6 - 7;
    Ezekiel 34:4 - 6; Luke 15:3 - 6; 1 Peter 2:25.)

    What are some of the reasons why we, like sheep, lose our way?

    How do we find our way back to the Shepherd?

2. Which path does the shepherd call his sheep to follow, and
    where does it lead? (See Psalms 23:3; 27:11; Proverbs 3:5 - 6;
    4:10 - 13.)

    How do we learn to follow the path of our Shepherd?

    Why do we have to submit to the Shepherd's will in order to
    walk the paths of righteousness with him?

3. What concern does God have for sheep who have lost their way, and what does he long for them to do? (See Jeremiah 6:16; 50:4 – 7.)

4. What does God promise to do when his sheep allow him to lead them in paths of righteousness? (See Psalm 23:3; Isaiah 49:8 – 10; Revelation 7:16 – 17.)

THINK ABOUT IT
Paths of Righteousness

In the open desert, thousands of narrow grazing trails form a maze of criss-crossing paths that are just close enough together that sheep and goats can reach the grass between them. With little rain to wash them away, some of these trails have existed since the time of Abraham. To walk on these paths

FORMED OVER MILLENNIA BY THE FEET OF SHEPHERDS AND THEIR FLOCKS, THESE GRAZING TRAILS IN THE NEGEV LIKELY EXISTED DURING THE TIME OF ABRAHAM.

continued on next page . . .

requires careful attention. Some paths gradually change direction. Others end suddenly at the edge of a cliff.

People who are unfamiliar with the paths in a specific desert area easily become lost. It is not surprising that the Bible speaks of lost sheep that wander off the "paths of righteousness" and can no longer find their shepherd. Fortunately, it is the shepherd's job to find them.

The Hebrew phrase translated "he [the LORD] restores my soul," in Psalm 23:3, conveys the sense of the Shepherd "bringing back" or "returning" wandering sheep that have taken the wrong path. The Shepherd brings them back to follow "paths of righteousness" that he knows lead to pasture, rest, and water. In the deserts of life, we too become lost and struggle to find the right path. But God our Shepherd is in the desert with us, and he calls out to us from the right path. If we trust him and obediently follow him, we will find that the path leads straight to the Shepherd and from there to the refreshment and restoration he provides.

Reflection

As we go through life's deserts we sometimes find ourselves on confusing and uncertain paths. We cannot see far ahead or know which route to take in order to handle our pain. Some paths may leave us wondering how we will survive. Yet even during these times, our Shepherd's voice is calling for us to follow him on the path he has chosen.

It is not easy to submit to God's will and purpose when he leads us through painful struggles. It took me (Ray) several months to accept that my heart attack was part of God's purpose to mold and shape me into the person he wanted me to be. When I finally accepted that he had a purpose in that desert, it became a doorway to peace and growth I had never experienced before. My choice to listen to his voice and follow him on the path of his choosing, although it was difficult, led to the pasture, water, and rest that he promises.

When have you, or someone you love, struggled with God because he allowed you to experience a painful "desert" time?

In what ways did you reject his role as your Shepherd? Why, and for how long?

What caused you to keep listening — or once again listen — for his voice and follow him, trusting that even if he led you on a difficult path he would be with you and provide for you?

In what ways did God shape you during that time into the person he desires you to be?

When have you lost your way during a painful desert experience and struggled to hear the voice of your Shepherd in order to stay on the right path?

What caused your feeling of loss and sense of overwhelming indecision and confusion?

How did you find your way back to the Shepherd and his path?

What did you learn through that experience to help you listen more carefully for your Shepherd's voice and enable you to keep walking with him on paths of righteousness?

How does having a faithful, loving Shepherd who will lead you on the right paths throughout your life encourage and strengthen you?

Memorize

He restores my soul.
He guides me in paths of righteousness
    for his name's sake.
Even though I walk
    through the valley of the shadow of death,
I will fear no evil,
    for you are with me;
your rod and your staff,
    they comfort me.

Psalm 23:3 – 4

THERE'S HOPE IN THE DESERT

Water was precious in ancient Israel (as it is to this day). Rain typically fell during five months of the year, and the Jordan River was Israel's only major river. For the people living in these lands, thirst was more than a temporary discomfort; it was a frightening, life-threatening reality.

People survived much of the year by using water that had been channeled into cisterns during the rainy season and stored. The most prized sources of water, however, were springs that mysteriously flowed out of the rock and provided what the Israelites called "living water" — fresh, flowing water. They considered these constant streams of water to be water that the Lord himself provided. Although they are very rare, springs in the desert were even more significant. When God's people were in the desert, these springs often made the difference between life and death.

Since 70 percent of the Promised Land is desert and some of the most significant events in Israel's history took place in desert regions, it is not surprising that biblical writers often included references to water, thirst, and cisterns. They also created powerful metaphors of desert and "living water" to describe the experiences of God's people and their relationship with their God. Thus the harsh realities of desert life often represent the difficult and painful times when God's people struggle to survive. In these "deserts" life is hard, so the presence of God portrayed as "living water" is not just a beautiful image, but it satisfies our desperate thirst and gives us life. People cannot thrive in the deserts of life without God's "living water."

Interestingly, the restoration of *shalom* — God's perfect peace, harmony — in the coming messianic age is distinguished by the absence of thirst. Consistent with the rest of Scripture, the prophetic vision God gave John is built on the reality that God alone satisfies the thirst that overwhelms his people in their deserts: "Never again will they hunger; never again will they thirst. The sun will not beat upon them, nor any scorching heat. For the Lamb at the center of the throne will be their shepherd; he will lead them to springs of living water. And God will wipe away every tear from their eyes" (Revelation 7:16 – 17).

Just as in ancient times when God provided precious water by rain, snow, and springs or by literally bringing water out of the rock when his people were in desperate need, he alone is the source of "living water" today. When his thirsty people call on him, he provides life-giving water. Whatever thirst we may experience in our deserts — physical, emotional, relational, or even spiritual — God promises to provide according to his will. Whenever we, like the panting deer or the thirsty desert traveler, cry out to him, he meets us in our deserts. He comes to us like a spring of "living water" and sustains us as we walk the desert path. Eventually our journey through earthly deserts will lead to heaven, the eternal Promised Land, where there will be no more deserts and no more thirst.

Opening Thoughts (3 minutes)

The Very Words of God

> On the last and greatest day of the Feast, Jesus stood and said in a loud voice, "If anyone is thirsty, let him come to me and drink. Whoever believes in me, as the Scripture has said, streams of living water will flow from within him."
>
> **John 7:37 – 38**

Think About It

Most of us have a vision of what we would like our life to be. Whether or not our present life matches our hope, we long to experience and feel certain things. In our relationship with God, for example, we long for true intimacy — to trust him, know him, walk with him, and enjoy the abundant and gracious provision he promises.

When you find yourself walking a desert path of suffering, hardship, or sorrow, what happens to your hope?

To what extent do the hardships of your path define your hope, perhaps even causing it to vanish like a drop of water on desert sand?

To what extent does your hope flow into your desert experience and shape your walk on the path?

DVD Notes (31 minutes)

God is in the desert

The right kind of feet

A thirst for living water

God is our En Gedi

We are En Gedi to other people

God's continuing provision

DVD Discussion (6 minutes)

1. On the map on page 283, locate En Gedi near the western shore of the Dead Sea. Notice how close the Judea Wilderness is to the more populated mountain areas of Hebron, Bethlehem, and Jerusalem. Why do you think the desert was such an effective tool for God to use in teaching the ancient Israelites? In teaching us today?

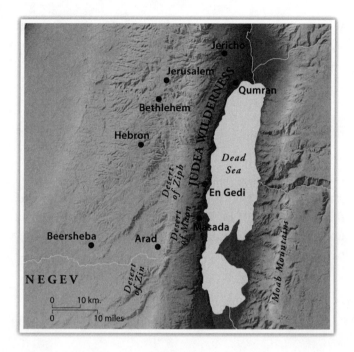

2. En Gedi, set against the backdrop of an extremely dry and rugged desert, is an amazing sight. How does the image of En Gedi being a sanctuary in the Judea Wilderness help you to picture God being a sanctuary in your deserts?

Does God's presence with you in your deserts make as great a difference as the springs of En Gedi do in the desert wilderness? Should it? Why or why not?

3. What are your thoughts about asking God to give us the right kind of feet to travel the paths he has chosen for us rather than asking him to make our paths easier?

4. Imagine choosing cistern water (remember the stagnant pools left after floods in the wadi?) over the fresh, clear, flowing waters of En Gedi! In what ways do we sometimes do this when we ignore God and the springs of living water he provides?

    How has this video helped you to see what we are really choosing when we make such a choice?

5. What have you discovered through this series of desert lessons that stands out in your mind as a picture of how God is with you and will express his love to you during your own desert experiences?

Small Group Bible Discovery and Discussion (14 minutes)

Living Water for All Who Thirst

When God's ancient people experienced life's painful, difficult deserts, they needed the hope of his presence and provision. During those times, as expressed in the figurative language of the Bible, God became their "rock," "shade," "shelter," "shepherd," "bread" — and "water." The water of God is "living water," fresh, flowing, invigorating water that he causes to flow out of even the hardest rock in the scorching desert. By drinking in his healing presence, symbolized by living water, his thirsty people find the strength to continue walking the path he has chosen for them. It is no different for us. We also experience painful, difficult deserts for which we need the healing presence of God's living water.

1. What is associated with God's presence in each of the following passages, and what does it provide for people in the desert? (See Genesis 2:8 – 10; Jeremiah 2:13; Revelation 22:1 – 2.)

    Since water is essential for sustaining physical life in the desert, what might be the consequence of turning away from the presence of God when we face desert experiences?

2. Which images did Isaiah use to describe the overflowing abundance of God's presence in the desert, and what would result from it? (See Isaiah 35:4 – 7.)

3. When Jesus spoke with the Samaritan woman at the well, what did he say about the thirst we experience in this broken world, and how does it differ from the living water he offers? (See John 4:10 – 14.)

As you think about your relationship with Jesus, how would you define the water that he offers, and how does a person "drink" it in?

4. During the Feast of Sukkot, during the time the prayers for water were offered, who did Jesus invite to come to him and why? (See Jeremiah 17:13; John 7:37 – 39.)

What amazing claim did he make in light of the prophet Jeremiah's words?

5. When we experience great thirst in life's deserts and come to Jesus to drink in his living water — his words, his love, and his presence — what do we become in relationship to other people? (See Isaiah 32:2.)

DATA FILE
The Feast of Sukkot

After the fall harvest, the Israelites celebrated the Feast of Sukkot (also called Feast of Booths, or Tabernacles). It was a time to be especially thankful for God's blessings. Following God's command, his people came to Jerusalem and built booths of olive, palm, and myrtle branches (Nehemiah 8:15) that provided shade. They were to leave enough space between the branches that they could see the sky and be reminded of their years in the desert. These booths (*sukkot*, plural: *sukkah*) gave the feast its name. For seven days, the people lived, ate, and slept in these booths and rejoiced before God, praising him for his gifts of freedom, land, and bountiful harvests.

Sukkot took place at the end of the dry season, and rain was needed immediately to ensure a bountiful harvest the following year. So the celebration of God's harvest was coupled with fervent prayers for next year's rain. During a special ceremony that included prayers for rain, priests marched from the temple to the pool of Siloam, which was fed by the "living water" flowing from the spring of Gihon. A priest filled a golden pitcher with water, and the procession returned to the temple. Then the priest solemnly poured this water into one of two silver funnels leading into the stone altar used for daily drink offerings. At this time, the people—accompanied by the levitical choir—began a chant that meant, "O Lord, save us by sending rain as well." Imagine the joyful noise!

During Sukkot, four huge menorahs (more than seventy-five feet tall) were erected in the women's court of the temple. These commemorated the small amount of sacred oil that burned miraculously for eight days in the menorah in the Holy of Holies after Judah Maccabee defeated the Greek army of Antiochus and reclaimed Jerusalem. Light from these could be seen from every house in Jerusalem.

In the context of Sukkot, the water ceremony, and the menorahs blazing with light, Jesus presented the message of his kingdom to great crowds thronging the temple in Jerusalem (John 7:10, 14). On the "last and greatest day of the Feast" (John 7:37), against the backdrop of the water ceremony, Jesus proclaimed: "If anyone is thirsty, *let him come to me* and drink. Whoever believes in me, as the Scripture has said, streams of living water will flow from within him" (John 7:37–38, emphasis added). His words must have had a stunning impact.

Faith Lesson (5 minutes)

Jesus knew well the thirst that overwhelms people in the desert. He came to live among us and offer us the living water that satisfies our thirst. He also willingly became thirsty on our behalf. In a poignant declaration of his own desert as he suffered on the cross, he said, "I am thirsty" (John 19:28; also Psalm 69:21).

Jesus is now reunited with the Father, but Matthew 25:31 – 46 suggests that he continues to identify with our deserts of hunger, thirst, nakedness, loneliness, and illness: "Whatever you did for one of the least ... you did for me" (Matthew 25:40). In response to these deserts, he wants those who follow him — those of us who have been filled to overflowing with his living water — to partner with him in bringing his *shalom* (peace, harmony) to our broken world. He wants us to live up to his promise (Isaiah 32:2; John 7:38) and be living water for people around us who suffer in the desert.

1. When your deserts overwhelm you, where do you turn for help, and how deeply do you drink the living water of Jesus' words, love, and presence?

    If you are drinking it, in what ways does it satisfy your thirst? If you are not drinking it, what keeps you from doing so?

2. How encouraging is it to you that Jesus also experienced the thirst of desert times, so that he knows both the struggle and pain of your physical needs and your spiritual thirst?

3. When have you been refreshed by living water from a person who walked closely with Jesus and was filled to overflowing with it? In what ways did God use that person to refresh and restore you?

    How great a priority is it for you to be living water for other people, and in what ways do you do this?

4. It is nearly impossible to imagine the spiritual desert, as evidenced by his thirst, that Jesus experienced when he was separated from God the Father because of the sins he bore on the cross for us. In what ways is a broken relationship with God a vast and dreadful desert?

    What does it mean to you that Jesus was willing to go into that desert in order to be living water for you?

5. When have you, or someone close to you, experienced a dreadful spiritual desert, and what difference did the living water of God make at the time?

How might you encourage people around you to drink the living water of Jesus so that they will never again experience the thirst of separation from God?

Closing (1 minute)

Read aloud John 4:14: "Whoever drinks the water I give him will never thirst. Indeed, the water I give him will become in him a spring of water welling up to eternal life."

Then pray together, thanking God for the living water of his presence that he provides for us in our deserts. Ask him to open your eyes to recognize opportunities to share God's living water with others through your words and actions. Thank him for the hope you have because he leads his people through the desert and into the Promised Land — eternal life in heaven with him.

Memorize

Whoever drinks the water I give him will never thirst. Indeed, the water I give him will become in him a spring of water welling up to eternal life.

John 4:14

Walking with God through Our Deserts

In-Depth Personal Study Sessions

Day One | Longing for God in the Desert

The Very Words of God

> *O God, you are my God,*
>   *earnestly I seek you;*
> *my soul thirsts for you,*
>   *my body longs for you,*
> *in a dry and weary land*
>   *where there is no water.*

Psalm 63:1

Bible Discovery

A Thirst for God

In the Bible, desert, drought, and thirst symbolize the difficult and painful times of suffering that we experience. As we endure these times, we become painfully aware of how much we long for the healing presence and merciful provision of God. When the Israelites suffered from a lack of water as they traversed the barren deserts of Sinai, for example, their suffering became a driving thirst that caused them to call out to God. In many respects the pain and turmoil of our passage through the dry and weary deserts of life can be like a driving thirst too. It can lead us to call out to God and makes the fresh, living water that he provides through his presence all the more refreshing and sustaining.

1. In Psalm 63:1, what thirst for God was David experiencing as he wrote this song in the desert? (Hint: Ponder such words as *my God, earnestly, seek, thirsts, longs, weary.*)

In what way(s) do these powerful words touch a chord in your heart and remind you of how much you desire God's presence when you pass through your deserts?

DATA FILE

Wilderness of Judea

The Judea Wilderness is not a desert of sandy hills. Beginning on the eastern slope of the Judea Mountains and descending into the Rift Valley in which the Dead Sea and the Jordan River are found, this desert is steep and mountainous. In a distance of about ten miles, the land descends from more than 3,000 feet above to more than 1,400 feet below sea level! Runoff from rains in mountains to the west has carved deep canyons into the soft limestone bedrock and makes travel through this desert challenging. The farther east one travels in this desert, the more arid and steep it becomes until it ends in cliffs above the Dead Sea.

THE MOUNTAINOUS DESERT OF THE JUDEA WILDERNESS

Bounded by the hill country of Ephraim to the north and the Negev desert to the south, the Judea Wilderness is thirty miles long and begins within sight of people who live in the central mountains. It is only a short, half-mile walk east of Bethlehem or Jerusalem to "go into the desert." Because of its proximity to the population centers of Israel, this desert has played a significant role in the history and spiritual development of the Jewish people.

The western edge of the Judea Wilderness receives enough rain to provide sufficient grazing, so it remains, as it was during ancient times, the land of shepherds and their flocks. The more rugged regions of the desert to the east became a place of refuge where David hid from Saul, John the Baptist isolated himself from the usual religious practices of his day, and the Essenes labored over their scrolls. It is also where Jesus faced the evil one. The Israelites were familiar with this desert either because they lived near it or walked through it on their way to Jerusalem for the annual festivals. So the biblical writers used images from the desert to describe life in relationship with God, especially the restoration of *shalom* to God's creation.

2. Even when we are suffering greatly in the midst of a desert experience, there's a part of us that wants to "solve" it ourselves — to "get tough" and dismiss our thirst as insignificant, to become angry that we are thirsty, to frantically pursue any drop of relief we can find. But God desires a close, intimate relationship with his people and promises to walk with us when we face such struggles. He wants us to make our needs, even the deepest longings of our heart, known to him so that he can respond. Isaiah 30:18 says, "The LORD longs to be gracious to you; he rises to show you compassion.... Blessed are all who wait for him!"

So set aside some time to thoughtfully and prayerfully read the following expressions of longing by people facing desert experiences. Learn from them and experience God's presence and provision in ways you may not have known before. As you complete the chart on page 294, (1) identify the kind of deserts these people apparently were facing and reflect on how they are similar to your own deserts; (2) notice how these people described their pain to the Lord and reflect on how you can express your needs to the Lord more intimately; and (3) notice how these people longed for God's presence and provision — as if they had been overcome with thirst — and reflect on God's goodness and how deeply you want to experience it.

Text	Their Desert	Description of Their Pain	Expression of Their Longing
2 Chron. 14:11			
Job 29:2−6			
Ps. 5:1−3, 8−9			
Ps. 33:18−22			
Ps. 40:13−17			
Ps. 42:1−5, 9−10			
Ps. 61:1−4			
Ps. 88:1−5			
Ps. 119:81−88			
Ps. 143:1−6			

Reflection

We all experience times when we are hot, weary, parched, and thirsty. We wish that our pain, struggles, doubts, fears, loneliness … would just go away. Often they don't. Time in the desert is hard, and sometimes it is hard for a long time. But in the scorching heat and silence of our suffering, God is there. He waits for you to long for his presence and express your needs to him because he longs to be gracious and show his compassion for you.

What desert in your life has nearly overcome you?

What deep needs and pain has it created in your life?

How do you long for God to provide, help, and care for you in this desert?

To what extent have you expressed your needs and longing to God, and how might you more openly and intimately share them with him?

In what ways — no matter how small — is God meeting your needs and longings in this desert?

Memorize

> *O Lord, be gracious to us;*
> > *we long for you.*
> *Be our strength every morning,*
> > *our salvation in time of distress.*

Isaiah 33:2

Day Two | The Feet of the Deer

The Very Words of God

> *It is God who arms me with strength*
> > *and makes my way perfect.*
> *He makes my feet like the feet of a deer;*
> > *he enables me to stand on the heights.*

2 Samuel 22:33 – 34

Bible Discovery

The Right Feet for Paths in the Desert

At a young age, David became an instant celebrity in ancient Israel. He was a shepherd from Bethlehem when Samuel anointed him to be Israel's next king. Through his brave step of faith and God's powerful strength, David killed Goliath and achieved national hero status. He was pressed into service as a harp-playing armor bearer for King Saul.

But David's popularity was short-lived. He was no longer a shepherd in the desert, but his desert experiences were not over. Saul was still king over Israel and became consumed with jealousy toward him, even using military power to pursue David in the desert wilderness.

Driven into the safety of the desert and apparently rejected by Israel, David must have felt that God's plans for his life were falling apart. It was a painful experience physically and emotionally. David longed for God's presence and provision to comfort and sustain him. During these years, he wrote psalms that for thousands of years have sustained God's people during painful times. His psalms reflect the desert times in his life when he learned to trust God to sustain him and to give him the "feet" to not only walk on God's paths but to do so in amazing ways.

1. Many of David's desert paths were incredibly difficult — full of symbolic and literal heat, rocky heights, enemies in hot pursuit, wadi floods, and other challenges. God didn't make David's desert paths smooth or remove him from the desert, but for the most part David was aware of God's presence with him. Second Samuel 22 gives us a glimpse into David's desert experiences and his relationship with God during that time. Read the chapter and then consider the following questions.

   a. What hard times did David face and which metaphors did he use to describe them? (See vv. 5 - 6, 17 - 19.)

   b. What did God do — literally and metaphorically — to enable this young man of faith to survive and fulfill his purpose amidst arduous and painful challenges? Note on the following chart ways in which God delivered David and provided just enough for him to endure his difficult path. (See vv. 7 - 20, 29 - 37, 40 - 46.)

God's Deliverance	God's Provision for a Difficult Path

c. Which metaphors did David use to describe the God in whom he trusted and what God had provided so that he could safely and quickly travel on the difficult, dangerous paths God had chosen for him? (See vv. 2–3, 29, 31–34, 47.)

THINK ABOUT IT

God Provides the Right Feet for the Desert

Negotiating the rugged mountains, deep canyons, and rocky ground of the Judea Wilderness is hard, dangerous work. The graceful ibex, however, are able to move with little effort on nearly impossibly steep trails at hazardous heights. They can do this because God, their Creator, gave them a soft hoof that grips the rock without slipping.

As he looked back on his desert experiences, David praised God for making his feet like the feet of a deer, which likely refers to the ibex. David didn't need God to make his path less difficult. Rather, he trusted God to lead him

THE IBEX IS AT HOME AMONG ROCKY, IMPOSSIBLY STEEP TERRAIN. THE SOFTNESS OF THEIR FEET GIVES IBEX SECURE FOOTING, WHICH ENABLES THEM TO MOVE OVER TREACHEROUS SLOPES WITH SPEED AND GRACE.

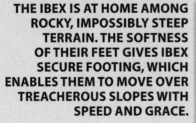

on the right path and to give him the right feet to walk it. David had learned an important desert lesson that applies to anyone who walks a difficult path: if God provides the right feet, any path is possible.

2. When we struggle in the desert, our thoughts often are consumed by the pain and hard work of surviving a rough, steep, rocky path. We may wish for our path to be smooth and easy, but we rarely think about the role our feet play on our journey. God, however, "will guard the feet of his saints" (1 Samuel 2:9). In what ways has God provided protection for the feet of his people in order to help them to walk painful, difficult, and even dangerous desert paths? (See Deuteronomy 29:5; Psalms 37:28 – 31; 40:1 - 2; 66:8 - 9; Habakkuk 3:17 - 19.)

Reflection

It is a challenge for those of us who follow Jesus in Western culture to grasp the perspectives of the biblical writers. Many of us live in abundance and often have everything we need and much of what we want, so we tend to associate physical abundance, comfort, and leisure with God's blessing. Some people even proclaim that God promises to provide such abundance to all who have faith. So when we experience times of suffering and loss, our faith wavers. We struggle to believe that God is still with us and still loves us. Although it is true that God often blesses his people with abundance, the Bible is clear that God also allows — and even leads — those who faithfully obey him to walk on difficult paths through life's deserts.

What do you imagine that David, who had been anointed to be Israel's next king, felt about his situation as he literally ran for his life on narrow, dangerous desert trails?

What do you think enabled him to handle his disappointment and confusion regarding the future path God had promised?

If you have been in a desert in which God's apparent purpose for your life fell apart and you found yourself alone and vulnerable, what sustained you during that time?

When David encountered difficult — even impossible — paths, and God gave him the "feet" to walk them with confidence and safety, how did David respond?

To what extent are you satisfied that God has provided the right "feet" for you to walk the painful and difficult paths in your life?

In what way(s) has God protected your feet as you have walked dangerous, desert paths, and why do you think he chose to do this rather than leading you on a flat, smooth, and easy path?

FOR GREATER UNDERSTANDING
Pray for the Right Feet!

For many years, I (Ray) would plead with God for easier, safer, smoother paths when I passed through the rugged and difficult terrain of life's deserts. Sometimes my paths became easier; other times they were more difficult. Some of my Jewish friends opened my eyes to a new way to pray during desert times. They prayed for God to provide what they needed to walk whatever path he determined was best. They wanted *his* path, even if it meant a desert path.

Their perspective reminded me of Jesus pleading with God to take away the cup of suffering awaiting him on the cross, yet submitting to God's will and walking the path that led to the cross.[1] Through his submission to suffering, Jesus learned obedience.[2] And that is what I want. I want to learn to seek the path God desires, not the easier one. So David's song in 2 Samuel 22:34 has become like a symphony in my heart. I can now say, "Lord, whatever path you choose as best for me, give me the right feet."

The ibex of En Gedi climb dangerous cliffs with breathtaking swiftness. They are the perfect reminder that no matter how difficult and painful the path may be, God has given them the right feet to walk it.

Day Three | In the Desert, God is Life!

The Very Words of God

> *"Be appalled at this, O heavens,*
> *and shudder with great horror," declares the* Lord.
> *"My people have committed two sins:*
> *They have forsaken me,*
> *the spring of living water,*
> *and have dug their own cisterns,*
> *broken cisterns that cannot hold water."*

Jeremiah 2:12 – 13

Bible Discovery

Life or Death? There Is No Other Choice

Without water, living things die. This is true in both the physical and spiritual sense. Just as God waters the earth to sustain the life of all living things, his presence and his Word are the living water that sustains the life and fruitfulness of the spirit. Nowhere is this more true than in the desert. When there are few oases and little rainfall, physical thirst forces desert travelers to be quite mindful of their water supply. In a similar way, we need to be mindful of our spiritual water supply in order to survive the deserts of life.

Just as God promised to bring his thirsty people, Israel, out of the desert and into a good land with flowing streams and springs, he promises to continuously supply our need for water even during the arid times of life. The spring at En Gedi, where this session was filmed, apparently has run without fail for more than 3,400 years! David drank from it during his time, and people still drink its refreshing water today. As it never fails, God never fails to supply springs of living water to those who follow him (Isaiah 58:11). But we have to choose to drink the living water God provides. Many people, it is sad to say — including some who profess to follow Jesus — choose water from a different source.

1. The metaphor of living water is rooted in the Israelites' desert experiences during the exodus to the Promised Land. As you read each of the following, try to imagine their situation. Think about the brutal heat and intense thirst they experienced. Think about the fear that they and their children would not survive. (See Exodus 15:22 - 27; 17:1 - 7; Numbers 20:1 - 11; Deuteronomy 8:15; Isaiah 48:21.)

    a. Can you imagine the wonder, amazement, and ecstatic joy they must have felt when they tasted the "sweet" water at Marah and at other times saw God's provision gush forth out of solid rock?

b. How did they know that the water came from the Lord?

c. God's provision did not deliver his people from the desert's hardships, but what did it do for them?

d. In what ways is God's provision of water for the Israelites in the desert similar to his provision of living water for your desert experiences?

e. Do you seek and appreciate God's provision of living water for you with the same wonder and enthusiasm that you imagine the Israelites felt when God provided water for them? Why or why not?

GOD'S GIFT OF WATER IN THE DESERT

DID YOU KNOW?
Cistern Water

It is a rare and thrilling sight to see clean, fresh-flowing spring water in the desert. Wherever God provides living water, abundant life will flourish. But much of the water available in the deserts of the Middle East is not the living water of God; it is cistern water.

Desert cisterns are essential, but they are not the most desirable water source. Cisterns are cut into the rock to store run-off rainwater. The water that flows into them carries dirt, animal droppings, and insects with it. Over time, leaves and even animals may fall into the cistern. So cistern water is not very clean.

Cisterns are also somewhat unreliable. Cut into porous limestone, they sometimes leak and always require regular repair and plastering. And if the rains have been inadequate, cisterns may dry up. What a contrast a cistern is to the clean, flowing water God longs to provide for his people.

2. In the following passages, what did God provide or promise to provide for people who were "thirsty" for his presence?

Text	God's Provision for Those Who Thirst
Ps. 107:4–9	
Isa. 41:17–20	
Isa. 44:3–5	
Isa. 49:8–10	
John 4:5–14	

Text	God's Provision for Those Who Thirst
Rev. 21:6	
Rev. 22:17	

3. What is God's assessment of people who fail to rely on his free gift of living water to sustain them and instead seek water from other sources? (See Jeremiah 2:11 – 13; 17:5 – 13.)

    Think about the language God used to criticize people who reject his gift of living water. Which other situations ignite such anger in him, and what does this say to you about the seriousness of rejecting his presence and provision?

    What do you think is the motivation behind our rejection of God's provision even when we are suffering in life's deserts?

Reflection

One of the rules for desert survival is to drink water *before* becoming thirsty. When we feel thirst, we are already depleted and can quickly become dangerously dehydrated. The solution is to keep drinking so that we never feel thirsty. In a sense we need to practice the same rule in relationship to God's living water so that we do not find ourselves dying of thirst in the heat of life's scorching deserts.

We may know it is important to pursue an intimate relationship with God and drink in his provision of "living water" regularly, but we often neglect doing it. In fact, the first thing we often sacrifice when life is stressful is our time with God. We run at a frantic pace, passing through deserts of stress, pain, loss, and hurt and become spiritually dehydrated — thirsty to the point of crisis. When this happens, we do more than place ourselves at risk. We greatly diminish the extent to which we can share God's "living water" with other people (John 7:38).

God desires that we drink his living water every day — whether or not it is a day in the desert. Before we find ourselves in life's deserts, we need to seek God and his "living water" regularly through the Bible, prayer, corporate worship, and relationships with other followers of Jesus. Then, when those desert times come, we will know where the springs of living water are, and we will be fully hydrated to face the heat of the desert paths on which God guides us.[3]

> During what time in your life's deserts have you received the living water of God's presence, and what did it, and does it, mean to you?

> In what ways have other people been affected by God's gift of living water during that time in your life?

> When have you in some way rejected God's living water and tried to drink your fill of "cistern water"?

To what extent were you aware of the choice you were making? When one young man on the Israel trip recognized the living water God offers, he exclaimed, "I have been drinking Dead Sea Water (twenty-five times more salty than the ocean) when the spring of En Gedi was right there!"

From which cisterns have you chosen to drink — alcohol, achievement, sex, popularity, acquisition of possessions — when you could have enjoyed God's living water?

What did you think you were providing for yourself that God would not provide for you?

God longs for people to drink deeply of his living water. What will you do from this time forward to fill yourself with his water daily so that you will become like an oasis of God's living water?

Memorize

This is what the Lord says:
"In the time of my favor I will answer you,
      and in the day of salvation I will help you;
I will keep you and will make you
      to be a covenant for the people,
to restore the land
      and to reassign its desolate inheritances,

to say to the captives, 'Come out,
  and to those in darkness, 'Be free!'
"They will feed beside the roads
  and find pasture on every barren hill.
They will neither hunger nor thirst,
  nor will the desert heat or the sun beat upon them.
He who has compassion on them will guide them
  and lead them beside springs of water."

Isaiah 49:8–10

Day Four | Meeting God in the Desert Sanctuary

The Very Words of God

O God, you are my God,
  earnestly I seek you;
my soul thirsts for you,
  my body longs for you,
in a dry and weary land
  where there is no water.
I have seen you in the sanctuary
  and beheld your power and your glory.

Psalm 63:1–2

Bible Discovery

Experiencing God's Presence in the Desert

Those of us who think like Westerners tend to view the desert in
terms of its physical properties — hot, dry, rocky, barren — and
how they affect us when we are there — overwhelmed, exhausted,
thirsty. But in the minds of God's ancient people, the deserts near or
in which they lived held great spiritual significance. So the inspired
biblical writers used the desert figuratively to describe various
dimensions of life and God's relationship to his people.

Many of God's people, including Abraham, Jeremiah, Elijah, and
Jesus spent time in the Judea Wilderness as did faithful Jews who
traveled through that desert to participate in the annual festivals in

Jerusalem. As God's people walked the difficult paths of that desert, they were reminded of God's promise to be their helper in times of trouble. Sending the scapegoat that symbolically removed the sins of the people into the Judea Wilderness was a representation of God's forgiveness and holiness. The promise that God will cause the desert to blossom in fertile beauty provided an image of hope that God's *shalom* will be restored. And for David, the Judea Wilderness also became *kadosh,* translated as "sanctuary" in Psalm 63:2, but also "holiness" or "holy" elsewhere.

1. David's experiences in the Judea Wilderness were by no means easy. What circumstances made his survival in the desert even more challenging, and in what ways did he experience more than just a physical desert? (See 1 Samuel 23:9 – 24:2.)

2. What was the time in the desert like for David? (See Psalms 18:1 – 6, 16 – 19; 41:1 – 2, 9 – 12; 86:11 – 17.)

   In what ways had God made his watchful presence known to David and shown him mercy and protection?

   What had David discovered about God, and how did he respond to God's provision for him?

3. David is believed to have been in the Judea Wilderness when he wrote Psalm 63. What descriptions of his condition indicate that he was in the desert? (See v. 1.)

4. After all that David had been through, would you have expected him to say that God had met him in the sanctuary — the holy place? Why or why not? (See Psalm 63:2.)

    As you consider what David experienced in the desert, what do you think made it a sanctuary for him?

    What do you think can make our desert experiences a sanctuary, a holy place where we meet God?

5. Generations before David spent time in the desert, Moses answered God's call from the burning bush in the desert of Sinai. Which words did God use to describe that place, and what did he ask Moses to do? (See Exodus 3:1 - 6.)

What impact do you think that encounter with God's holiness had on Moses as he answered God's call and led the Israelites out of Egypt, through the desert, and into the Promised Land?

Reflection

At first glance, it may be surprising that many people of the Bible experienced God deeply amidst the hardships and daily challenges of the desert. For them, the desert became a sanctuary — a holy place where they walked with God, talked with God, and grew to demonstrate their love for him through obedience to his every word. David described that time of intimacy with God as "my soul *clings* to you" (Psalm 63:8, emphasis added). The word translated "clings" is the same word used to describe the relationship of a man and woman in marriage (Genesis 2:24). So in his difficult desert, David knew the sweet, intimate embrace of God's presence and continually desired it.

In what way(s) have you experienced *sanctuary* — the sweetness of God's holy presence and provision — during a desert in your life?

If you have not experienced the sweetness of God's presence and provision, why do you think that is?

What do you think transforms a difficult desert into a holy place where the presence of God brings peace, comfort, and intimacy in the midst of pain and suffering?

Would you say that you lovingly "cling" to God in the desert you face? If not, which word(s) would you use to describe your relationship with him?

When you are in a desert experience, what causes you to praise God?

Memorize

O God, you are my God,
  earnestly I seek you;
my soul thirsts for you,
  my body longs for you,
in a dry and weary land
  where there is no water.
I have seen you in the sanctuary
  and beheld your power and your glory.
Because your love is better than life,
  my lips will glorify you.
I will praise you as long as I live,
  and in your name I will lift up my hands....
Because you are my help,
  I sing in the shadow of your wings.
My soul clings to you;
  your right hand upholds me.

Psalm 63:1 – 4, 7 – 8

Day Five | The Desert Path Leads Us Home

The Very Words of God

> *See, a king will reign in righteousness*
> *and rulers will rule with justice.*
> *Each man will be like a shelter from the wind*
> *and a refuge from the storm,*
> *like streams of water in the desert*
> *and the shadow of a great rock in a thirsty land.*
>
> Isaiah 32:1 – 2

Bible Discovery

God's Living Water Flows to All Who Are Thirsty

During their forty-year journey through the desert, the Israelites matured in their relationship with God. His presence lived among them in a portable tent shrine, the tabernacle, and as they received the living water that he provided in the midst of their hardships his partnership with them deepened. In the Promised Land, the Israelites built the temple as the permanent home for God's presence. Then Jesus, God incarnate, came to live among us and identified himself as the living water that satisfies the thirst of all who come to him. And on Pentecost, God's people became the new temple in which God lives by his Spirit.[4] God's presence no longer lives in one place; his community of people has become his dwelling place, taking his presence into the entire world. Consider what that means for us as we walk through our deserts and encounter other people on the desert path.

1. What does Isaiah 32:1 – 2 say each person in the kingdom of the righteous king (according to Jewish thought, the coming Messiah) will be, and how is this like what God promises to be for his people when they are in the desert?

2. God has not abandoned his people in the desert; he has not abandoned his world in chaos. He is not a wadi that floods in season; he is not a cistern that slowly runs dry. He is an ever-flowing spring of living water that provides relief from the thirst that overwhelms us in the desert. He desires that those who drink deeply of his living water will become streams of living water to other thirsty wanderers. What are some of the practical ways we can be like streams of living water to people who suffer in life's deserts? List them! (See Isaiah 58:6–12.)

    What results in the world and in our lives when we, as God's people, fulfill our role in the desert?

    What specific actions will you take to be like God's living water to people you encounter on your path?

    Can you be living water for another person when you are in the desert? Why or why not?

3. What did Jesus say to his followers in order to emphasize what those of us who have tasted God's living water are to be and do? (See Matthew 10:42.)

4. The promise of living water provides great hope for those of us who travel through the deserts of life, but that is just the beginning. The hope and healing restoration of *shalom* that God's living water brings to our desert experiences does not end with this life.

   a. What does the trickle of God's living water in Ezekiel's hope-filled vision become and accomplish, and in what ways is it a portrayal of *shalom*? (See Ezekiel 47:1 – 12.)

THE SPRINGS OF EN GEDI BRING LIFE-GIVING WATER INTO A BARREN DESERT.

b. When Jesus invited thirsty people to come to him and drink his living water, what would they receive and become, and how was this demonstrated at Pentecost? (See John 7:37 – 39; Acts 2.)

c. What can God's people count on experiencing in eternity? (See Revelation 7:11 – 17; 22:1 – 5.)

Reflection

As we faithfully walk through life's deserts, we have the opportunity to develop an intimate relationship with God and to drink deeply of his living water. God certainly gives his living water for our benefit, to provide relief for our suffering in the desert, but his gift is not exclusively for our benefit. God is gracious and generous with us because he wants us also to provide for those who are hurting. His desire is that as we are filled we will become streams of living water and bring hope, help, relief, and refreshment to others who suffer in life's deserts. Just as the oasis at En Gedi has sustained and blessed people for millennia, providing a taste of God's *shalom* in the midst of a harsh and difficult desert, he calls those of us who have received his living water to be like the oasis at En Gedi for other desert travelers.

How deeply does it touch you that God wants not only to bless you with living water, but wants you to be like him for others — a bubbling, life-giving spring of living water in a desert wasteland?

What is your commitment to finishing your remaining earthly journey well and being like En Gedi to other desert travelers?

What will you do to ensure that you do not cut yourself off from God, your source of living water?

What role does your community of faith play in helping you to find and receive God's living water and to be a channel of his living water to others who suffer in the desert?

How might you be encouraged and strengthened on your desert journey by spending time with people who are like fruitful gardens and provide an unfailing source of God's living water? Who do you know who is like this?

Can you be a stream of living water in the desert without actually living in the desert? Why or why not?

In what ways might your desert experiences, painful as they have been or may be right now, prepare you to be living water for people who also walk difficult desert paths?

How much hope do you find in the truth that one day, if you follow Jesus, you will complete your earthly journey and your path will lead you to eternity in the presence of God?

If Jesus is your Lord and Savior, what comfort and joy do you feel in knowing that when you complete your earthly journey, your path will lead you to your eternal home in the presence of God where there will be no more desert and you will never again thirst?

Memorize

They are before the throne of God
    and serve him day and night in his temple;
and he who sits on the throne
    will spread his tent over them.
Never again will they hunger;
    never again will they thirst.
The sun will not beat upon them,
    nor any scorching heat.
For the Lamb at the center of the throne will be their shepherd;
    he will lead them to springs of living water.
And God will wipe away every tear from their eyes.

Revelation 7:15 – 17

NOTES

Session 2: It's Hot Here and There's No Way Out

1. Song of Songs 8:5 (English Standard Version).

2. Genesis 32:23; 1 Samuel 17:40; 30:9; 1 Kings 17:5 – 7.

3. I am indebted to a former teacher, Dr. Jim Fleming, for this insight. See *www.biblicalresources.net* for many of the outstanding resources he has produced for those who wish to better understand the Bible in the context in which God placed it.

4. This title is related to the shoot and branch from the line of David (see Isaiah 11:1; 53:2). Also see Matthew 2:21 – 23, where Jesus is to be called a Nazarene because he was from Nazareth. Both words descend from the Hebrew *netzer*, meaning "shoot" or "root" or "branch."

5. James W. Fleming, *Desert Spirituality* (LaGrange, Ga.: Biblical Resources, 2002). Fleming's description of God's use of desert experience to deepen his relationship with his people and strengthen their complete dependence on him is exceptional.

Session 3: Help Is Here

1. An excellent treatment is found in chapter 1 of *Eat This Book* by Eugene Peterson (Grand Rapids: Eerdmans, 2006).

Session 4: When Your Heart Cries Out

1. See Kenneth Bailey, *Jacob and the Prodigal* (Downers Grove, Ill.: InterVarsity Press, 2003), for an excellent description of the use of metaphor to present theological truth.

Session 5: They Were Not Wandering

1. Lois Tverberg explains the biblical use of the metaphor of path in an article entitled "M'agal: Righteous Paths," at En-Gedi Resource Center, *www.egrc.net*.

Session 6: Ears to Hear

1. For a helpful outline of the Bible's use of this metaphor, see "Sheep, Shepherd" in Leland Ryken, James C. Wilhoit, and Tremper

Longman III, *Dictionary of Biblical Imagery* (Downers Grove, Ill.: InterVarsity Press, 1998).

2. See Nogah Hareuveni, *Desert and Shepherd in Our Biblical Heritage* (Neot Kedumim, 1991) for an excellent discussion of the shepherds of the Bible lands.

3. "Water in the Desert," *The Jerusalem Post*, May 19, 2006. Rabbi Shlomo Riskin is the chief rabbi of Efrat and chancellor of Ohr Torah Stone Colleges and widely respected. His publications include an excellent two-volume set: *Torah Lights: Genesis Confronts Life, Love and Family* and *Exodus Defines the Birth of a Nation* (Jerusalem: Urim Publications, 2005).

Session 7: There's Hope in the Desert

1. Mark 14:36.

2. Hebrews 5:8.

3. Thanks to Lois Tverberg for this excellent insight into how desert and living water must inform our daily walk. See En-Gedi Resource Center, *www.egrc.net*.

4. Isaiah 2:3; 1 Corinthians 3:16–17; Ephesians 2:19–22.

ACKNOWLEDGMENTS

The people of God set out on a journey, a journey from bondage to freedom, a journey to the Promised Land, a place flowing with milk and honey. A simple journey, really: leave Egypt and walk to the Promised Land. All they had to do was cross the Sinai Desert and they were there. It would not take long; it was only two hundred miles. But God had another route planned. During the forty years that journey took, the Hebrews, concerned about themselves as we all are, became a community — a people who would put the Creator of the universe on display for a broken world.

The production of this study series is also the work of a community of people. Many contributed of their time and their talent to make it possible. Recognizing the work of that unseen community is to me an important confirmation that we have learned the lessons God has been teaching his people for three thousand and more years. It takes a community. These are the people God has used to make this entire series possible.

The Prince Foundation:

The vision of Elsa and Ed Prince — that this project that began in 1993 would enable untold thousands of people around the world to walk in the footsteps of the people of God — has never waned. God continues to use Elsa's commitment to share God's story with our broken world.

Focus on the Family:

> Clark Miller — chief strategy officer
> Robert Dubberley — vice president, content development
> Paul Murphy — manager, video post production
> Cami Heaps — associate product marketing manager
> Anita Fuglaar — director, global licensing

Carol Eidson — assistant to business affairs director
Brandy Bruce — editor

That the World May Know:

Alison Elders, Lisa Fredricks — administrative assistants

Chris Hayden — research assistant. This series would not have been completed nor would it have the excellence of content it has without his outstanding research effort.

The Image Group and Grooters Productions:

Mark Tanis — executive producer
John Grooters — producer/director
Amanda Cooper — producer
Eric Schrotenboer — composer/associate producer
Mark Chamberblin, Adam Vardy, Jason Longo — cinematography
Dave Lassanke, Trevor Lee — motion graphics
Drew Johnson, Rob Perry — illustrators
Sarah Hogan, Judy Grooters — project coordinators
Ken Esmeir — on-line editor and colorist
Kevin Vanderhorst, Stephen Tanner, Vincent Boileau — post-production technical support
Mark Miller, Joel Newport — music mixers
Keith Hogan, Collin Patrick McMillan — camera assistants
Andrea Beckman, Rich Evenhouse, Scott Tanis, Kristen Mitchell — grips
Shawn Kamerman — production assistant
Marc Wellington — engineer
Juan Rodriguez, Paul Wesselink — production sound
Ed Van Poolen — art direction

Zondervan:

John Raymond — vice president and publisher, curriculum
Robin Phillips — project manager, curriculum
Mark Kemink — marketing director, curriculum

T. J. Rathbun — director, audio/visual production

Tammy Johnson — art director

Ben Fetterley — book interior designer

Greg Clouse — developmental editor

Stephen and Amanda Sorenson — writers

BIBLIOGRAPHY

To learn more about the cultural and geographical background of the Bible, please consult the following resources.

Bailey, Kenneth. *Jacob and the Prodigal*. Downers Grove, Ill.: InterVarsity Press, 2003.

Beitzel, Barry J. *The Moody Atlas of Bible Lands*. Chicago: Moody Press, 1985.

Berlin, Adele, and Marc Zvi Brettler. *Jewish Study Bible*. Philadelphia: Jewish Publication Society and New York: Oxford University Press, 2004.

Bible Land Trees. New York: Jewish National Fund, n.d. *www.bible-landtrees.com/PageIn.asp?info_id=1036*. (Accessed 14 September 2010.)

Bivin, David. *New Light on the Difficult Words of Jesus: Insights from His Jewish Context*. Holland, Mich.: En-Gedi Resource Center, 2005. *www.egrc.net*.

Borowski, Oded. *Daily Life in Biblical Times*. Atlanta: Society of Biblical Literature, 2003. *www.sbl-site.org*. (Accessed 14 September 2010.)

Bottéro, Jean, Elena Cassin, and Jean Vercoutter, eds. *Near East: The Early Civilizations*. New York: Delacorte Press, 1967.

Clements, Ronald, ed. *The World of Ancient Israel: Sociological, Anthropological, and Political Perspectives*. Cambridge: Cambridge University Press, 1991.

DeJong, George. *In a Word: Lessons from the Language of the Wilderness*. Holland, Mich.: Under the Fig Tree Ministries, 2009. *www.underthefigtree.org*. (Accessed 14 September 2010.)

Dickson, Athol. *The Gospel According to Moses*. Grand Rapids: Brazos Press, 2003.

Edersheim, Alfred. *The Temple: Its Ministry and Services as They Were at the Time of Jesus Christ*. London: James Clarke & Co., 1959.

_____. *The Life and Times of Jesus the Messiah*. Peabody, Mass.: Hendrickson, 1993.

Elbaum, Leiah. *Plants of the Bible*. Leiah Elbaum, ed. N.p., 2003. *http://natureisrael.com/plants2002.html*. (Accessed 14 September 2010.)

Feiler, Bruce. *Walking the Bible: A Journey by Land through the Five Books of Moses*. New York: HarperCollins, 2002.

Fleming, James W. *Desert Spirituality*. LaGrange, Ga.: Biblical Resources, 2002. *www.biblicalresources.net*. (Accessed 14 September 2010.)

_____. *The Explorations in Antiquity Center*. LaGrange, Ga.: Biblical Resources, 2007. *www.biblicalresources.net*. (Accessed 14 September 2010.)

Fretheim, Terence E. *Exodus: Interpretation, A Bible Commentary for Teaching and Preaching*. Louisville: John Knox Press, 1991.

Friedman, Richard Elliot. *Commentary on the Torah*. San Francisco: Harper, 2001.

Hareuveni, Nogah. *Nature in Our Biblical Heritage*. Kiryat Ono, Israel: Neot Kedumim, 1980.

_____. *Tree and Shrub in Our Biblical Heritage*. Kiryat Ono, Israel: Neot Kedumim, 1980.

_____. *Desert and Shepherd in Our Biblical Heritage*. Lod, Israel: Neot Kedumim, 1991.

Hartman, Craig. *Through Jewish Eyes*. Greenville, S.C.: JourneyForth Books, 2010.

Hepper, F. Nigel. *Illustrated Encyclopedia of Bible Plants*. Grand Rapids: Baker, 1992.

Hoffmeier, James K. *Ancient Israel in Sinai*. Oxford: Oxford University Press, 2005.

_____. *Israel in Egypt*. Oxford: Oxford University Press, 1996.

Kamhi, Ellen, ed. "Herbs of the Bible." *The Natural Nurse*. N.p., n.d.

Levenson, Jon D. *Creation and the Persistence of Evil*. Princeton, N.J.: Princeton University Press, 1988.

_____. *Sinai and Zion: An Entry into the Jewish Bible*. San Francisco: Harper, 1985.

Levine, Baruch A. *The JPS Torah Commentary: Leviticus*. Philadelphia: Jewish Publication Society, 1991.

Magness, Jodi. *The Archaeology of Qumran and the Dead Sea Scrolls*. Grand Rapids: Eerdmans, 2002.

Maier, Paul L., trans. *Josephus: The Essential Works*. Grand Rapids: Kregel, 1988.

Martinez, Florentino Garcia. *The Dead Sea Scrolls Translated: The Qumran Texts in English*. Grand Rapids: Eerdmans, 1996.

Milgrom, Jacob. *The JPS Torah Commentary: Numbers*. Philadelphia: Jewish Publication Society, 1991.

Modzelevitch, Martha, ed. "Flowers in Israel: Acacia tortilis." N.p., 2005. *www.flowersinisrael.com/Acaciatortilis_page.htm*. (Accessed 14 September 2010.)

Murphy-O'Connor, Jerome. "Triumph Over Temptation." *Biblical Archaelogy Review* (August 1999). *www.bib-arch.org.*

Musselman, Lytton J. "Trees in the Koran and the Bible." FAO Corporate Document Repository, Food and Agricultural Organizations of the U.N., 2003. *www.fao.org/docrep/005/y9882e/y9882e11.htm*. (Accessed 14 September 2010.)

Notley, R. Steven. "Are You the One Who Is to Come?" CD of workshop given at the En-Gedi Resource Center, Holland, Mich., 2002. *www.egrc.net.*

Peterson, Eugene. *Eat This Book*. Grand Rapids: Eerdmans, 2006.

Pixner, Bargil. *With Jesus Through Galilee According to the Fifth Gospel.* Rosh Pina, Israel: Corazin Publishing, 1992.

Plants of the Bible. Norfolk, Va.: Old Dominion University, 2006. *www.odu.edu/~lmusselm/plant/bible/acacia.php*. (Accessed 14 September 2010.)

Pryor, Dwight. *Unveiling the Kingdom of Heaven*. Dayton, Ohio: Center for Judaic-Christian Studies, 2008.

Rainey, Anson F., and R. Steven Notley. *The Sacred Bridge: Carta's Atlas of the Biblical World.* Jerusalem: Carta, 2006.

Riskin, Shlomo. *Torah Lights: Genesis Confronts Life, Love and Family.* Jerusalem: Urim Publications, 2005.

_____. *Torah Lights: Exodus Defines the Birth of a Nation*. Jerusalem: Urim Publications, 2005.

_____. *Torah Lights Volume 2: Exodus Defines the Birth of a Nation.* Urim Publications, 2006.

Ryken, Leland, James C. Wilhoit, and Tremper Longman III, *Dictionary of Biblical Imagery*. Downers Grove, Ill.: InterVarsity Press, 1998. See articles on "Chaos," "Wilderness," "Peace," and "Wasteland."

Sarna, Nahum. *The JPS Torah Commentary: Exodus*. Philadelphia: Jewish Publication Society, 1991.

_____. *The JPS Torah Commentary: Genesis*. Philadelphia: Jewish Publication Society, 1991.

_____. *Exploring Exodus: The Origins of Biblical Israel*. New York: Schocken Books, 1996.

Schiffman, Lawrence H. *Reclaiming the Dead Sea Scrolls*. New York: Doubleday, 1995.

Shanks, Hershel. "Searching for Essenes at Ein Gedi, Not Qumran." *Biblical Archaeology Review* (July/August 2002).

Shanks, Hershel, ed. *Understanding the Dead Sea Scrolls*. New York: Vintage Books, 1993.

Silverman, David P. *Ancient Egypt*. Oxford: Oxford University Press, 1997.

Smith, William (Rusty Russell, ed.). *Smith's Bible Dictionary*. Gresham, Ore.: Bible History Online. *www.bible-history.com/smiths/S/Shittah+tree.+Shittim*. (Accessed 14 September 2010.)

Spangler, Ann, and Lois Tverberg. *Sitting at the Feet of Rabbi Jesus*. Grand Rapids: Zondervan, 2009.

Swenson, Allan. *Plants of the Bible: And How to Grow Them*. New York: Citadel Press, 1995.

Telushkin, Rabbi Joseph. *The Book of Jewish Values*. New York: Bell Tower, 2000.

Tigay, Jeffrey H. *The JPS Torah Commentary: Deuteronomy*. Philadelphia: Jewish Publication Society, 1991.

Tverberg, Lois, with Bruce Okkema. *Listening to the Language of the Bible*. Holland, Mich.: En-Gedi Resource Center, 2004. *www.egrc.net*.

VanderKam, James C. *The Dead Sea Scrolls Today*. Grand Rapids: Eerdmans, 1994.

_____. *The Meaning of the Dead Sea Scrolls*. San Francisco: Harper Collins, 2004.

Vermes, Geza. *Complete Dead Sea Scrolls in English*. New York: Penguin Group, 1998.

Wilkinson, Richard H. *The Complete Gods and Goddesses of Ancient Egypt*. Hong Kong: Thames and Hudson, 2003.

_____. *The Complete Temples of Ancient Egypt*. Hong Kong: Thames and Hudson, 2000.

Willard, Dallas. *The Divine Conspiracy*. San Fransisco: Harper, 1997.

Wilson, Marvin. *Our Father Abraham: Jewish Roots of the Christian Faith*. Grand Rapids: Eerdmans, 1989.

Young, Brad H. *Jesus the Jewish Theologian*. Peabody, Mass.: Hendrickson, 1995.

More Great Resources
from Focus on the Family®

Volume 1: Promised Land

This volume focuses on the Old Testament—particularly on the nation of ancient Israel, God's purposes for His people, and why He placed them in the Promised Land.

Volume 2: Prophets and Kings of Israel

This volume looks into the nation of Israel during Old Testament times to understand how the people struggled with the call of God to be a separate and holy nation.

Volume 3: Life and Ministry of the Messiah

This volume explores the life and teaching ministry of Jesus. Discover new insights about the Son of God.

Volume 4: Death and Resurrection of the Messiah

Witness the passion of the Messiah as He resolutely sets His face toward Jerusalem to suffer and die for His bride. Discover the thrill the disciples felt when they learned of His resurrection and were later filled with the Holy Spirit.

Volume 5: Early Church

Capture the fire of the early church in this fifth set of Faith Lessons™. See how the first Christians lived out their faith with a passion that literally changed the world.

Volume 6: In the Dust of the Rabbi

"Follow the rabbi, drink in his words, and be covered with the dust of his feet," says the ancient Jewish proverb. Come discover how to follow Jesus as you walk with teacher and historian Ray Vander Laan through the breathtaking terrains of Israel and Turkey and explore what it really means to be a disciple.

Volume 7: Walk as Jesus Walked

Journey to Israel where the 12 disciples walked the walk their rabbi Jesus taught them. Examining the culture and the politics of the first century, Ray Vander Laan opens up the Gospels as never before.

FOR MORE INFORMATION

Online:
Go to FocusOnTheFamily.com
In Canada, go to FocusOnTheFamily.ca

Phone:
Call toll-free: 800-A-FAMILY (232-6459)
In Canada, call toll-free: 800-661-9800

FOCUS®
ON THE FAMILY

BD10XTTWMK

More Great Resources
from Focus on the Family®

Volume 8: God Heard Their Cry

Just when it seemed that Pharaoh could not be defeated, God provided for His people in ways they never could have imagined. Join historian Ray Vander Laan in ancient Egypt for his study of God's faithfulness to the Israelites—and a promise that remains true today.

Volume 9: Fire on the Mountain

When the Israelites left Egypt, they were finally free. Free from persecution, free from oppression, and free to worship their own God. But with that freedom comes a new challenge—learning how to live together the way God intends. In this ninth set of Faith Lessons™, discover how God teaches the Israelites what it means to be part of a community that loves Him, and the lessons we can begin to live out in our lives today.

Volume 10: With All Your Heart

Do you remember where your blessings come from? In Exodus, God warned Israel to remember Him when they left the dry desert and reached the fertile fields of the promised land. But in this tenth volume of Faith Lessons™, discover how quickly the Israelites forgot God and began to rely on themselves.

Volume 11: The Path to the Cross

Discover how the Israelites' passionate faith prepares the way for Jesus and His ultimate act of obedience and sacrifice at the cross. Then, be challenged in your own life to live as they did—by every word that comes from the mouth of God.

Share Your Thoughts

With the Author: Your comments will be forwarded to the author when you send them to *zauthor@zondervan.com.*

With Zondervan: Submit your review of this book by writing to *zreview@zondervan.com.*

Free Online Resources at
www.zondervan.com

Zondervan AuthorTracker: Be notified whenever your favorite authors publish new books, go on tour, or post an update about what's happening in their lives at www.zondervan.com/authortracker.

Daily Bible Verses and Devotions: Enrich your life with daily Bible verses or devotions that help you start every morning focused on God. Visit www.zondervan.com/newsletters.

Free Email Publications: Sign up for newsletters on Christian living, academic resources, church ministry, fiction, children's resources, and more. Visit www.zondervan.com/newsletters.

Zondervan Bible Search: Find and compare Bible passages in a variety of translations at www.zondervanbiblesearch.com.

Other Benefits: Register yourself to receive online benefits like coupons and special offers, or to participate in research.

ZONDERVAN

ZONDERVAN.com/
AUTHORTRACKER
follow your favorite authors